Security for Automotive Electrical/Electronic (E/E) Architectures

TECHNISCHE UNIVERSITÄT MÜNCHEN

Lehrstuhl für Realzeit-Computersysteme

Security for Automotive Electrical/Electronic (E/E) Architectures

Philipp Mundhenk

Vollständiger Abdruck der von der Fakultät für Elektrotechnik und Informationstechnik der Technischen Universität München zur Erlangung des akademischen Grades eines

Doktor-Ingenieurs (Dr.-Ing.)

genehmigten Dissertation.

Vorsitzender:	Prof. Dr.-Ing. Georg Sigl
Prüfer der Dissertation:	1. Prof. Dr. sc. Samarjit Chakraborty
	2. Assoc. Prof. Suhaib A. Fahmy, PhD School of Engineering, University of Warwick, United Kingdom

Die Dissertation wurde am 16. Juni 2016 bei der Technischen Universität München eingereicht und durch die Fakultät für Elektrotechnik und Informationstechnik am 01. Juni 2017 angenommen.

Bibliografische Information der Deutschen Nationalbibliothek
Die Deutsche Nationalbibliothek verzeichnet diese Publikation in der Deutschen
Nationalbibliographie; detaillierte bibliografische Daten sind im Internet über
http://dnb.d-nb.de abrufbar.
1. Aufl. - Göttingen: Cuvillier, 2017
   Zugl.: (TU) München, Univ., Diss., 2017

© CUVILLIER VERLAG, Göttingen 2017
   Nonnenstieg 8, 37075 Göttingen
   Telefon: 0551-54724-0
   Telefax: 0551-54724-21
   www.cuvillier.de

   ISBN 978-3-7369-9604-5
   eISBN 978-3-7369-8604-6

Acknowledgements

This thesis results from research performed at TUM CREATE, Singapore in collaboration with Technische Universität München (TUM), Germany and Nanyang Technological University (NTU), Singapore. The following people had significant impact on this research and without them, this thesis would not have been possible.

I would like to especially thank my advisors from TUM and NTU, Samarjit Chakraborty and Suhaib A. Fahmy for their supervision and advise when undertaking this thesis. Their insights into the processes and feedback helped shape the work leading to the thesis presented here, as well as the thesis itself.

Furthermore, I extend my deepest gratitude to Martin Lukasiewycz and Sebastian Stein-horst, whose involvement in this work allowed continuous immediate feedback at any time and who had a large impact on both this work and me personally.

I would also like to thank my colleagues Matthias Kauer, Peter Waszecki, Florian Sagstetter, Daniel Zehe, Swaminathan Narayanaswamy, and Shreejith Shanker for constructive discussions on my work and bearing with me throughout the time at TUM CREATE. I enjoyed the work with Andreas Ettner and Artur Mrowca, who I had the pleasure to supervise and who both did excellent work. Furthermore, the collaborations with Andrew Paverd, Sidharta Andalam, and Kai Xiang Wang led to some very interesting work, which, without their contributions, would not have been possible. Last but not least, I would like to thank the EVA team and project manager Daniel Gleyzes. The experience of building a fully functional electric vehicle from scratch is an incredible one, unique in every possible way, and I will never forget the time in this project and the experiences gained.

Finally, I would like to thank my fantastic wife Lee Hui Xin, as well as my sister Anna and my parents Angela and Ulrich Mundhenk for their support and understanding throughout my studies, especially in stressful phases where time was short.

While this is only a short list, many more people, institutions, and companies have contributed to and laid the basis on which this chapter of my education, experience and life is built. There are far too many to be mentioned in this short section. I am grateful for every single one of those.

Thank you!

Abstract

The increasing connectivity among vehicles increases their attack surface and challenges their security. This thesis explores approaches to improve analysis and design of security for in-vehicle networks. Therefore, a design time security analysis, a runtime authentication and authorization framework, and a flexible scheduling scheme, efficiently enabling security on FlexRay are presented. The infotainment system of an electric taxi is introduced as a design experience to demonstrate the necessity of new approaches in automotive security.

Vehicles today include a large number of electronics in form of Electronic Control Units (ECUs). These ECUs are interconnected in internal vehicle networks implementing distributed control tasks. With the trend of rising interconnectivity and the Internet of Things (IoT), these in-vehicle networks are increasingly connected to other vehicles and the Internet. While the internal vehicle networks are shielded with gateways and firewalls, these protection mechanisms are not impenetrable. As for these external interfaces the same protection mechanisms as on the Internet are used, the same types of attacks can be applied. Once having access to the vehicle network, an attacker often has as many possibilities for influence as the vehicle owner or an authorized workshop. These internal networks consist of specialized automotive components, are often not sufficiently segmented or secured, and messages are transmitted unencrypted.

Combining security and automotive real-time systems is challenging in many ways. The heterogeneity and complexity of automotive communication systems and their interconnections make the quantification of security a difficult task. Lower computational capabilities and network bandwidth, coupled with the real-time behavior in automotive systems makes implementation of computation and bandwidth intensive security challenging. New solutions are required to address security in the automotive domain in context of not only functional, but also real-time requirements.

This thesis explores approaches to (1) analyze security of in-vehicle networks at design time, (2) secure network traffic efficiently through authentication and authorization at runtime, and (3) enable security on legacy communication systems. These approaches are motivated in context of the infotainment system of an electric taxi. The interaction of passengers with the infotainment system opens an attack vector on safety-critical in-vehicle systems and requires security to be a priority.

The first approach targets the problem of quantifying the security of architectures and forms the basis for evaluation of all other approaches. It is not straightforward to evaluate the security of a network. No method to quantify the security of automotive networks currently exists. In this thesis, the Security Analysis for Automotive Networks (SAAN) is proposed. SAAN uses probabilistic model checking to calculate the security of automotive networks, based on the architecture and expert evaluations of components. Evaluations of SAAN prove its capabilities to detect security flaws and compare automotive architectures in terms of security. SAAN employs an automotive-specific model generation, taking into account the specific security dependencies in the automotive architecture. These dependencies are formulated as rules and form the basis for state-space reduction in the model. By reducing the model size, the performance of the model checking can be improved by two to three orders of magnitude over state of the art model generation.

After establishing the ability to analyze networks for security, the second approach is centered around securing in-vehicle network traffic efficiently. To secure traffic, it is required to authenticate communication participants and authorize messages. This is typically ensured by authentication frameworks. Traditional authentication frameworks have high computation and bandwidth requirements, incompatible with automotive networks. This thesis proposes the Lightweight Authentication for Secure Automotive Networks (LASAN). LASAN is specifically tuned to the automotive environment, leveraging on the fixed network structure to reduce evitable flexibility in the protocols and minimize message sizes and thus bandwidth requirements. Splitting asymmetric and symmetric protocol components distributes the computational requirements and thus reduces the delays in time-critical phases of the system. Evaluations show improvements of setup latency of two to three orders of magnitude over the state of the art. Besides improved efficiency, LASAN can be easily integrated with existing automotive processes, such as Over-The-Air (OTA) updates or workshop maintenance and repair.

The third approach targets the problem of security in legacy communication systems. Existing time-triggered communication systems, such as FlexRay, are highly limited in their flexibility regarding message lengths and transmission times. This limits the entropy available for security, allowing brute-force attacks on cryptographic keys, effectively rendering employed security mechanisms useless. The policy-based scheduling for FlexRay presented in this thesis enables a higher flexibility for messages on the bus by abstracting the bond between time-triggered slots and messages. Messages are flexibly arranged in a virtual communication layer, before being divided into slots. Thus, messages can be transmitted priority-based and messages longer than one slot lengths can be transmitted. This allows the implementation of authentication frameworks and increases the available entropy per message through enlargement, supporting encryption efficiently. Through the underlying time-triggered system, worst-case response times can be calculated efficiently. Evaluations show improvements in message transmission latencies by close to one order of magnitude over conventional FlexRay scheduling. At the same time, flexibility for message sizes and periods is increased significantly.

The security approaches in this thesis are closely linked. Without a flexible message transmission scheme, authentication protocols cannot be implemented. Without an evaluation option for security, quantifying the impact of an authentication framework is highly complicated. Without an authentication framework, secure setup of architectures is not possible. The proposed approaches spans across both the design time and runtime aspects of automotive communication system development. A tight integration is key to security in automotive networks. This thesis lays the groundwork for this.

Zusammenfassung (German Abstract)

Die zunehmende Vernetzung von Fahrzeugen erhöht auch deren Angriffsfläche gegenüber Manipulationen und bringt neue Herausforderungen für deren Informationssicherheit (Automotive Security) mit sich. Diese Dissertation stellt Ansätze zur Verbesserung des Designs und der Analyse von Fahrzeugnetzen vor. Es werden eine Sicherheitsanalyse zur Entwurfszeit, eine Authentifizierungs- und Authorisierungsmethodik zur Laufzeit und ein flexibler Scheduling-Ansatz zur effizienten Implementierung von Sicherheit auf FlexRay vorgestellt. Um den Bedarf neuer Ansätze im Bereich Automotive Security zu demonstrieren, wird das Infotainmentsystem eines elektrischen Taxis als Fallstudie vorgestellt.

Aktuelle Fahrzeuge beinhalten eine große Anzahl elektronischer Steuergeräte, sogenannte Electronic Control Units (ECUs). Diese Steuergeräte sind über fahrzeuginterne Netzwerke verbunden um verteilte Steuerungsaufgaben zu realisieren. Durch die zunehmende Vernetzung und das Internet der Dinge (Internet of Things, IoT) werden diese internen Fahrzeugnetze immer häufiger mit anderen Fahrzeugen und dem Internet verbunden. Obwohl die internen Kommunikationsnetze in vielen Fällen mit Firewalls und Gateways abgeschottet sind, so können diese Schutzmechanismen doch umgangen werden. Da für diese externen Verbindungspunkte die gleichen Schutzmechanismen wie für Geräte im Internet eingesetzt werden, sind diese auch für die gleichen Attacken empfänglich. Sobald ein Angreifer diese Barrieren überwunden und Zugang zu den internen Fahrzeugnetzen hat, hat dieser oft genauso viele Möglichkeiten der Einflussnahme wie der Besitzer des Fahrzeugs oder eine autorisierte Werkstatt. Die internen Fahrzeugnetze bestehen aus speziellen automobilen Systemen und sind oft nicht ausreichend segmentiert und gesichert. Nachrichten werden meist unverschlüsselt übertragen.

Die Kombination von Sicherheit und automobilen Realzeitsystemen birgt viele Herausforderungen. Die Varianz und Komplexität automobiler Kommunikationssysteme und deren Verbindungen erschweren die Quantifizierung der Sicherheit deutlich. Geringere Prozessorleistung und Datenraten, in Kombination mit dem benötigten Realzeitverhalten in automobilen Systemen, erschweren die Implementierung von Sicherheit deutlich, da diese oft sehr rechen- und bandbreitenintensiv ist. Neue Lösungen sind nötig um Sicherheit im automobilen Bereich nicht nur funktional, sondern auch mit korrektem Realzeitverhalten umzusetzen.

In dieser Dissertation werden Ansätze vorgestellt um (1) die Sicherheit von internen Fahrzeugnetzen zur Entwurfszeit zu analysieren, (2) Datenübertragungen zur Laufzeit effizient zu authentifizieren und autorisieren und (3) Sicherheit auf existierenden Kommunikationssystemen zu etablieren. Diese Ansätze werden im Zusammenhang des Infotainmentsystems eines elektrischen Taxis erläutert. Dort eröffnet die Einbindung von Passagieren in das System eine

Angriffsmöglichkeit auf sicherheitsrelevante interne Fahrzeugsysteme und erfordert daher die Priorisierung der Absicherung des Systems.

Der erste in dieser Arbeit vorgestellte Ansatz fokussiert sich auf die Quantifizierung der Sicherheit von Fahrzeugarchitekturen und kann damit als Grundlage zur Evaluation aller weiteren Ansätze dienen. Sicherheit in Netzwerken zu evaluieren ist nicht trivial. Derzeit existiert keine Evaluationsmöglichkeit fuer die Sicherheit in automobilen Netzwerken. Aus diesem Grund wird in dieser Dissertation die „Security Analysis for Automotive Networks" (SAAN) vorgestellt. Basierend auf der Netzwerkarchitektur und der Bewertung einzelner Komponenten durch Sachverständige nutzt SAAN probabilistic Model Checking, um die Sicherheit von automobilen Netzen zu berechnen. Die Fähigkeiten von SAAN, Sicherheitslücken zu finden und die Sicherheit automobiler Architekturen zu vergleichen wird durch Evaluation des Ansatzes bestätigt. SAAN nutzt eine spezielle, auf den Automobilbereich angepasste Modellgenerierung, welche die spezifischen Sicherheitsabhängigkeiten in automobilen Architekturen berücksichtigt. Diese Abhängigkeiten werden als Regeln definiert und bilden die Basis zur Reduktion des Zustandsraums. Durch die Reduzierung der Modellgröße wird die Laufzeit des Model Checkings gegenüber dem Stand der Technik um zwei bis drei Größenordnungen verbessert.

Nachdem die Möglichkeit zur Sicherheitsanalyse von Netzwerken etabliert ist, konzentriert sich der zweite im Rahmen dieser Arbeit entwickelte Ansatz auf die effiziente Absicherung des Datenverkehrs im Fahrzeug zur Laufzeit. Um diesen Verkehr abzusichern, ist es erforderlich, die Kommunikationspartner zu authentifizieren und die Nachrichtenübertragungen zu autorisieren. Dies wird üblicherweise durch Authentifizierungssysteme erreicht. Existierende Authentifizierungssysteme haben hohe Anforderungen an Rechenleistung und Datenrate, welche nicht mit automobilen Netzwerken kompatibel sind. In dieser Dissertation wird deshalb „Lightweight Authentication for Secure Automotive Networks" (LASAN) vorgestellt. LASAN ist speziell auf die automobile Umgebung angepasst und nutzt die starre Netzwerkstruktur in automobilen Netzen zur Reduktion nicht benötigter Flexibilität. Gleichzeitig wird die benötigte Nachrichtengröße minimiert. Diese Maßnahmen reduzieren die benötigte Bandbreite. Durch das Trennen von asymmetrischen und symmetrischen Protokollkomponenten wird die Rechenlast zeitlich verteilt und damit Verzögerungen in zeitkritischen Phasen des Systems minimiert. Die Evaluation des Ansatzes zeigt Verbesserungen der Latenz im Kommunikationsaufbau von zwei bis drei Größenordnungen im Vergleich zum Stand der Technik. Neben den Effizienzverbesserungen erlaubt LASAN eine einfache Integration in den automobilen Lebenszyklus und unterstützt damit beispielsweise Over-The-Air (OTA) Updates oder Wartung und Reparaturen.

Der dritte in dieser Arbeit vorgestellte Ansatz beschäftigt sich mit dem Problem der Sicherheit in existierenden Kommunikationssystemen. Existierende zeitgesteuerte Kommunikationssysteme wie FlexRay sind in ihrer Flexibilität bezüglich Nachrichtenlänge und Übertragungszeiten sehr limitiert. Dies begrenzt die Entropie, welche für Sicherheitsmaßnahmen zur Verfügung steht, und erlaubt damit Brute-Force-Angriffe auf kryptografische Schlüssel. Hierdurch werden die eingesetzten Sicherheitsmaßnahmen wertlos. Das in dieser Dissertation präsentierte „Policy-based Scheduling for FlexRay" erlaubt mehr Flexibilität für Nachrichten auf dem Bus, indem die Verbindung zwischen Zeitschlitzen und Nachrichten abstrahiert wird. Nachrichten werden flexibel in einer virtuellen Kommunikationsebene angeordnet, bevor diese in Zeitschlitze geteilt wird. Auf diese Weise können Nachrichten sowohl prioritätsbasiert als auch mit Nachrichtenlängen von mehr als einem Zeitschlitz übertragen werden. Dies erlaubt die Implementierung von Authentifizierungssystemen und erhöht die zur Verfügung stehende Entropie pro Nachricht, was wiederum effiziente Verschlüsselung ermöglicht. Durch das zugrunde liegende zeitgesteuerte System können die maximalen Laufzeiten für Nachrichten effizient berechnet werden. Auswertungen zeigen, dass Latenzen bei der Übertragung von Nachrichten im Vergleich zu Standard FlexRay um nahezu eine Größenordnung verringert werden können. Gleichzeitig erhöht sich die Flexibilität von Nachrichtengrößen und -perioden signifikant.

Die Ansätze in dieser Dissertation sind eng miteinander verbunden. Ohne ein flexibles Nachrichtenübertragungssystem können Authentifizierungssysteme nicht implementiert werden. Ohne Evaluationsmöglichkeiten ist es sehr kompliziert den Einfluss von Authentifizierungssystemen auf die Sicherheit zu bestimmen. Ohne Authentifizierungssystem ist es nicht möglich eine Architektur sicher einzurichten. Die vorgestellten Ansätze erstrecken sich somit sowohl über Entwurfs- als auch Laufzeitaspekte der Entwicklung von automobilen Kommunikationssystemen. Eine enge Integration ist der Schlüssel zu Sicherheit in automobilen Netzwerken. Diese Dissertation schafft eine Basis hierfür.

Contents

1

Introduction

Vehicles today contain a large number of assistant and entertainment functions. These functions are realized as electronic components running control software. Such electronics are used throughout the vehicle, covering all functional domains. Advanced Driver Assistance Systems (ADASs) such as lane keeping and braking assistants, as well as autonomous vehicles rely heavily on software, processing the input of sensors distributed around the vehicle and computing actions to take for the actuators in the vehicle. In case of a lane keeping assistant, the sensor input might originate from a camera system. An ECU processes this input, computes how much the steering needs to be actuated and sends appropriate commands to the steering wheel motor. Today, such functions are core elements in the vehicle, both from a safety, as well as a business perspective. On the one hand, these systems can avoid accidents, on the other, they heavily influence the decision of the customer to buy or forgo a vehicle [142].

To achieve the required functionality, multiple sensors, actuators and computational units (ECUs) need to be interconnected. The sensors and actuators are typically attached to ECUs as well, for filtering, pre-computation and encoding of data [139]. The networks, or Electric/Electronic (E/E) architectures, existing in vehicles today have been designed at times when vehicles were single, non-interconnected units. In recent years, this has changed significantly, as vehicles are equipped with Internet connections, WiFi, cellular (3G, 4G) and vehicle-to-X (v2X) connections, among others. Nowadays, most vehicles on the market have some sort of interconnection. While the internal networks slowly develop to adjust to these new requirements, they have not been designed with security in mind. Attacks on single vehicles, as well as attacks on vehicle fleets over Internet connections are becoming a reality [107]. The interconnection of insecure vehicle networks to the Internet is reminiscent of the interconnection of the first computer networks to the Internet and the resulting security issues in the 1980s. However, the security in vehicle networks is on many levels more concerning than the security in personal computer systems, as the vehicle networks and the connected ECUs have direct influence on the safety of the vehicle and its passengers.

The goal of this thesis is to advance secure communication in vehicles by contributing approaches for analysis and design of secure communication. The security of vehicles is analyzed and improvements are suggested based on the experience gained by designing and constructing the electric taxi EVA. EVA is a purpose-built electric taxi for tropical megacities developed and built in TUM CREATE. The lessons learned when securing the vehicle networks in EVA will motivate the remainder of the thesis, showing how to secure the communication in vehicle networks and how to evaluate this security. Furthermore, the challenges with security in the existing communication system FlexRay are outlined and one approach to solve these is shown.

In this chapter, the basic knowledge of automotive communication systems and network security is conveyed. Further, the challenges existing when combining these two domains are laid out. The detailed contributions of this thesis and the integration with existing work are shown.

1.1   Automotive Electrical/Electronic (E/E) Architectures

To understand the challenges to security in vehicles, the basic networking mechanisms need to be understood. In the following, an overview over E/E architectures in vehicles with a focus on existing and upcoming automotive bus systems is given.

Typically, automotive communication systems follow a bus structure (see Figure 1.1(c)). In many cases, these buses are interconnected by a central gateway in a star architecture (see Figure 1.1(a)). This concept is slowly changing, however, due to the introduction of functional *domains*, headed by a domain controller and interconnected over a backbone, typically in conjunction with a central gateway (see Figure 1.1(b)). The chosen architecture depends on the complexity, bandwidth and real-time requirements of the vehicle (see Section 1.1.1). Only recently, bus systems with sufficient bandwidth for backbone networks have been developed (see Section 1.1.3) [142].

The ECUs in vehicle architectures take up diverse tasks, from sensing tire pressure over user inputs via buttons to computations for systems such as Anti-lock Braking System (ABS) or Electronic Stability Program (ESP), and actuation of motor and brakes, among many others. ECUs will be shortly explored in Section 1.1.2.

1.1.1   Requirements

Based on the functions the vehicle network is to perform, the requirements on software and hardware for ECUs and communication systems can be defined [103]. Note that some of the requirements depend on the type of application. Some examples will be given in the following.

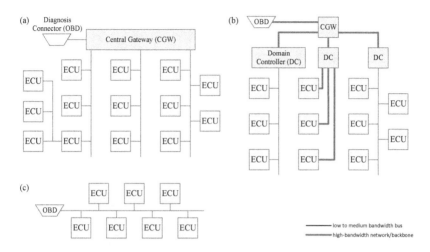

Figure 1.1: *Comparison of architecture variants: (a) Hierarchical bus systems with central gateway, (b) division into functional domains with domain controllers (DC), high-bandwidth backbone and central gateway (CGW) and (c) traditional single bus system.*

Cost. The overarching concern for vehicle architectures is cost. The minimization of cost for all components is key from the perspective of business model of the Original Equipment Manufacturers (OEMs) where revenues rise with lower production cost. Within this work, however, cost is not the main consideration. Whenever possible, cost is considered, e.g. by the reuse of existing elements, but this thesis is focused on the technical point of view on vehicle networks.

From the technical point of view, automotive architecture requirements can be characterized by their bandwidth demand, real-time capabilities, as well as number of devices, or, on a higher abstraction level, number of functions. In the following, we will quickly explain these requirements, before describing implementations addressing these requirements in more detail in the next section.

Bandwidth. Note that bandwidth demand strongly depends on the organization of the architecture. The drivetrain domain, e.g., typically requires less bandwidth than the infotainment domain. Overall, bandwidth demand in vehicle architectures is rising sharply and strongly driven by ADASs and infotainment systems. With an increasing amount of cameras and other data intensive sensors such as Lidar, the required bandwidth for data transmissions rises quickly. When transmitting High-Definition (HD) video data, as required by assistance systems such as lane keeping assistants, data rates of 1 to 18 MBit/s are required for a single camera, depending on resolution, encoding, frame rate, etc. Traditional bus systems, such as shown in Figure 1.1(c) are in many cases not able to cope with such bandwidth demand. These networks have been designed to transmit control data, which in most cases is limited to messages of less than 2 Bytes length per application and data rates of less than 1 kBit/s per stream. Thus, new architectures and networks have been developed, allowing to segregate traffic and use these sensors and systems, without interfering with safety-critical control data. The most common of these networks will be discussed in Section 1.1.3.

Real-Time. Automotive systems require real-time data transmissions and processing, such that signals arrive and actions are taken guaranteed within a given time. This is to ensure that safety-critical functions can be executed as intended, without delay. An ABS, e.g., requires response times in the range of milliseconds to ensure that the vehicle remains steerable. These requirements originate in the potentially high speed of the vehicle and the frequency of actions required to fulfill a function. With increasing speed, longer response times or retransmissions of messages translate to a longer distance traveled before an action is taken. This can have potentially fatal consequences, e.g. when emergency braking is applied to stop the vehicle before crashing into the end of a traffic jam. Other applications, e.g., those where user interaction is required, require less rigorous response times, as the user reacts in slower time intervals. The infotainment is one example for such applications.

Size. Last but not least, the architecture requirements are defined by the number of functions and, corresponding to this, the number of devices. In short, the size of the architecture has a large influence on its structure. While for low-end cars with a minimal amount of electronics, a single Controller Area Network (CAN) bus might be sufficient, high-end cars with requirements for bandwidth and real-time varying with the function, might require a hierarchical system, including some high bandwidth buses. It is important to note that with multi-core processors and generally more powerful ECUs being introduced into the automotive domain, the trend of *ECU consolidation* is picking up speed. Due to the large number of ECUs, the overhead in weight, energy consumption and cost in vehicles is not negligible anymore. With ECU consolidation, the OEMs move away from the concept of ECU per function and start integrating multiple functions onto one ECU. Thus, the number of ECUs is remaining stable or even reduced, while the number of functions is increasing.

After a quick overview of the automotive domain, highlighting the bandwidth, real-time and size requirements on architectures, the following section will discuss ECUs in more detail.

1.1.2 Computation

Due to the distributed nature of sensors, controllers and actuators and the high degree of concurrency, automotive networks can be considered complex, heterogeneous, and distributed computers [139]. Each computation component is running on a single ECU and ECUs are distributed spatially in the vehicle. The computational capabilities of these ECUs vary widely. On the higher end are engine control units, infotainment systems and the central controllers for ADASs, often containing modern multi-core processors with large amounts of main memory. These systems are, in their computational capabilities, comparable to modern consumer electronics [121, 123]. Unix-based Operating Systems (OSs) such as QNX [136] represent the main OSs for infotainment systems.

Devices with lower computational capabilities reach down to 8-Bit processors [122, 138]. Core clock frequencies of these devices are in the range of two-digit Megahertz or below. Memory reaches down to single-digit Kilobytes. These devices are typically used for small switching tasks, such as recognizing or triggering simple on/off switches, triggering of motor controllers, etc. Often, such devices are used in subsystems, which might be attached to the main networks via bridges.

Between these two extremes, nearly all sizes and types of devices can be found in vehicles today [142]. When dimensioning software to be used on all devices in the vehicle, such as security mechanisms, any performance estimation must take this diverse network nature into account. This makes it difficult to exactly quantify the computational capabilities of the overall vehicle network.

ECU consolidation. As the number of ECUs in current vehicles is in the upper double-digit range, OEMs have started to combine ECUs [22]. This process of reducing the number of ECUs by combining multiple tasks on a single, more powerful ECU is called ECUs consolidation. It is especially useful for pure controller ECUs. ECUs which need to access hardware components, such as a switches or motors can not be integrated easily without cabling overhead. By removing the medium size ECUs and integrating them with high powered ECUs, the distribution of ECUs in automotive networks is changing. In the future, one can expect networks with more high-powered and less medium size ECUs, with the number of low-power ECUs remaining in similar numbers, possibly rising slowly in the high-end market.

Security in ECUs. Not all computation of an ECU is performed in the Central Processing Unit (CPU). Additional computation units allow the efficient computation of specific functions. Examples for this are, e.g., graphics accelerators (Graphics Processing Unit (GPU)) for devices with screens and cryptographic accelerators. Especially cryptographic accelerators are important in the context of this thesis. Larger and partially also mid-range ECUs are often equipped with cryptographic co-processors. While hardware accelerators allow storage of cryptographic keys and can accelerate some encryption functions [62], co-processors provide a full computation environment, mirroring the main system, including secure memory, external device connections, etc. [5]. As modern microcontroller cores often integrate hardware accelerators and co-processor functions, many ECU CPUs are available with cryptographic hardware support at similar price points [5, 123].

1.1.3   Current and Upcoming Networks

This section will introduce the interconnections between these ECUs. The most common communication systems used in vehicles are introduced here. While this list is not exhaustive, it covers the largest part of automotive systems in use today.

Controller Area Network (CAN).   CAN is the most popular among the automotive bus systems [142]. It has been developed in the 1980s and has been standardized and extended by the International Organization for Standardization (ISO) in ISO 11898 parts 1-3 [57, 58, 59]. With bandwidths of between 125 kBit/s and 1 MBit/s and up to 8 Bytes per data packet, it allows the transmission of small amounts of status and control data in the vehicle. The CAN bus extension ISO 15765-2 defines segmentation of messages, thus allowing to transmit larger messages than 8 Bytes [66]. This is especially useful for diagnosis information. The success of CAN is in not small part founded in its cost, which is significantly lower than for most other systems on the market today.

CAN does not use direct addressing of receivers or identification of senders. Message frames do not include sender or receiver addresses and senders of messages can not be easily identified on the bus. Instead, receivers filter the traffic on the bus for accepted CAN message identifiers (IDs). Thus, the message ID is used as an indirect address.

CAN uses an arbitration mechanism to ensure access to the bus. Arbitration is achieved through the electrical characteristics of the bus, where a logical 0 on the bus is called dominant and overrides a logical 1. This way, the IDs of messages transmitted at the same time will be arbitrated automatically and the lowest message ID will pass.

While CAN is still the main prevailing system, the changing requirements towards more electronic functions, such as advanced driver assistance functions, require an increasing amount of bandwidth that CAN cannot cope with. Here, new communication systems are required.

Local Interconnect Network (LIN).   While CAN is already on the lower end in terms of cost, it is still undercut by Local Interconnect Network (LIN) [142]. LIN has been developed by the LIN Consortium in the 1990s as a very inexpensive communication system for simple switching operations or for the transmission of minimal diagnosis information. LIN is currently a standard under development by the ISO as ISO 17987 parts 1-7 [77]. With up to 20 kBit/s, the available bandwidth is significantly lower than CAN. A single message frame holds between 2 and 8 Bytes of data. The bus access is controlled by a single master node, requesting slave nodes to transmit as required. Similar to CAN, identification is achieved via message IDs. LIN is often used to connect a single or a small set of nodes in a subnetwork to a CAN device.

FlexRay.   FlexRay is a mixed system of time-triggered and event-triggered communication [142]. It is standardized as ISO 17458 parts 1-5 [69, 70, 71, 72, 73]. With a bandwidth of 10 MBit/s, it offers significantly higher transmission rates than CAN. Its time-triggered part, the static segment, allows transmissions to be aligned to a common time, synchronized across the whole network. This can significantly reduce the worst-case response time and is critical for systems that need to react fast, e.g. to guarantee the safety of vehicles. Due to the time in the static segment being divided into timeslots, the bus access is already defined at design time. The dynamic segment of FlexRay uses a Flexible Time Division Multiple Access (FTDMA) approach, providing access to the bus in timeslots, which ECUs might extend as required, thus implementing a priority scheme.

Through the timeslots in the static and dynamic segment, an implicit addressing scheme is implemented. As all devices are time synchronized, transmitters and receivers can send and receive in timeslots assigned at design time.

FlexRay has gained popularity quickly, due to it being able to ensure fast response times in the network. In domains such as the drivetrain of the vehicle, where worst-case response times are crucial for safety, FlexRay offers significant advantages. However, due to the precise timing requirements and the complexity of FlexRay, the price per controller is relatively high, compared to CAN. Furthermore, depending on the configuration of static and dynamic segment, as well as the utilization of both segments, the net bandwidth can be significantly lower than 10 MBit/s.

In 2013, FlexRay has been standardized as ISO 17458-1 to -5 and is now under the administration of ISO. FlexRay will be introduced in more detail in Chapter 5, where it is extended to carry large messages, allowing to implement the security measures proposed in this thesis.

Media Oriented Systems Transport (MOST). In the infotainment domain, the Media Oriented Systems Transport (MOST) bus is sometimes used [142]. MOST is specified by the MOST Cooperation specifies bandwidths of 25 and 150 MBit/s over optical cables and 50 and 150 MBit/s over copper cables [109]. As MOST can offer a relatively large bandwidth, it is ideal to be used in the infotainment domain, where larger amounts of data, e.g. audio and video streams, need to be transmitted across the network.

MOST uses a ring architecture and for safety-critical environments can be configured in a double ring structure to achieve redundancy. Each MOST bus contains a timing master, generating frames for timing synchronization for other nodes. The bus access is also controlled by this timing master, leaving space in the frames for asynchronous or synchronous data to be transmitted in so called channels.

The MOST bus is a rather complex communication system, which results in high effort and cost for design and implementation. In recent years, MOST is increasingly under pressure by Automotive Ethernet, which offers similar bandwidth at a lower price point.

While the automotive networks in the previous section have been around for many years, the automotive networking landscape is changing. The rise of ADASs, as well as infotainment functions, which require a high amount of data, led to the development of faster networks. Cameras are becoming more ubiquitous in vehicles and the use of their data in control systems often requires uncompressed images. Existing bus systems are not capable of transmitting sufficient amount of data for high resolution cameras.

Controller Area Network with Flexible Data-Rate (CAN FD). CAN FD is an enhancement of the traditional CAN bus and included in the 2015 version of the CAN standard [76]. It is fully compatible with CAN and can by used on the same physical connections.

CAN FD defines a new frame format, utilizing two different clocks for different parts of the frame. By keeping the clock for the frame headers at the same speed as for conventional CAN, compatibility can be achieved. However, in the data segment, the clock is increased up to 8-fold, allowing to transmit up to 64 Bytes per frame. This increases the bandwidth of CAN FD significantly, compared to CAN.

Some additional changes have been added to invalidate CAN FD frames for CAN transceivers on the same network, as these will otherwise not be able to accommodate and handle the increased clock and amount of data. Further, to allow error correction of the larger amount of data, new polynomials for the Cyclic Redundancy Check (CRC) have been defined.

Due to its similarities with CAN in terms of design, timing, as well as cost, CAN FD might become the ideal replacement for the slow and aged CAN bus in many vehicle domains that do not require multiple 10 MBit/s bandwidth and are more relaxed in terms of real-time constraints, like the comfort domain.

In this thesis, CAN FD is used to implement an authentication and authorization framework (see Chapter 4).

Automotive Ethernet. Ethernet is the de facto standard for wired consumer electronics [52]. Ethernet itself and derivatives of it have found their way into other domains, such as avionics [108] and industrial automation [49]. However, in the automotive domain, the conventional 8-wire, shielded Ethernet cables required would add to much cost and weight. Furthermore, modern Ethernet has a fundamentally different network topology, using point-to-point connections on the physical layer, instead of a bus. Ethernet has thus until recently only been used in very limited applications, such as an additional diagnosis connector, besides the mandatory On-Board Diagnosis (OBD)-II port [65].

This changed with the development of the BroadR-Reach PHY by Broadcom, announced in late 2011 and picked up for licensing by the One-Pair Ether-Net (OPEN) Alliance [127]. Further standardization of the technology in the Institute of Electrical and Electronics Engineers (IEEE) working groups for Ethernet (802.3) is in progress [54, 55]. In the following, the terms Automotive Ethernet and BroadR-Reach, referring to these technologies and standards will be used synonymously.

The BroadR-Reach technology allows to operate a conventional duplex 100 MBit/s connection over two wires, without the need for additional shielding. This technology is in use in vehicles on the road today, mostly to handle larger amounts of sensor data from sensors such as radar, Lidar and cameras. Due to the rising resolution of these sensors, car manufacturers are looking towards 1 GBit/s Ethernet connections, which could be employed for such sensor networks or to satisfy the increasing backbone traffic requirements [54].

BroadR-Reach targets the physical layer, reducing the weight and cost requirements of the communication medium. The Medium Access Control (MAC) and higher layers are not defined in these standards. When using Ethernet for safety-critical systems with real-time requirements however, the conventional approach for collision resolving on Ethernet is not ideal. In conventional Ethernet, when a collision occurs, the bus is blocked by participants for a short while, overriding the collided messages with a predefined pattern. Then, random back-off timers are started on both colliding senders, after which transmissions are started again. With these additional delays for collided messages and random back-offs, it is impossible to calculate reasonable worst-case response times. Furthermore, as all message on Ethernet have equal priority, priorities as they exist in vehicle networks today could not be implemented. Multiple approaches have been and are under development to tackle these issues, among them Audio Video Bridging (AVB) and Time-Sensitive Networking (TSN), shortly explained in the following.

Audio/Video Bridging (AVB). AVB (IEEE 802.1BA) has been developed for the entertainment domain, allowing synchronized recording and playback of audio and video without the need for dedicated cables per stream [51]. Furthermore, AVB offers the possibility to give priority to certain messages, via the Quality of Service (QoS) tag in the Ethernet frame, as defined in IEEE 802.1Q [53]. This standard has quickly gotten the attention of the automotive industry, as well as other industries, requiring time-synchronized real-time streams. However, the requirements of the automotive industry are stricter than the guarantees given by AVB. This lead to the development of TSN.

Time Sensitive Networking (TSN). TSN is the follow-up standard to AVB and developed by the same IEEE task group [56]. The standard is currently still under development. In comparison to AVB, TSN does set significantly stricter requirements for response times. Among others, TSN is expected to allow preemption of messages by higher priority messages, thus reducing response times. It is furthermore expected that TSN will allow dynamic reservation of streams at runtime.

1.2 Security

This section focuses on security aspects auf automotive architectures. Security in digital communications is not a new topic. In consumer networks and on the Internet, security has long been playing an important role and many standards have been developed, used and improved upon. The basic principles of these security mechanisms will be detailed in the following.

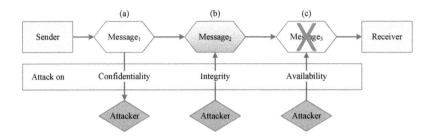

Figure 1.2: *The security principles of Confidentiality, Integrity and Availability in the context of messages on a communication system. In case of an attack on Confidentiality an attacker might be able to read a message (a). In case of an attack on Integrity an attacker can alter a message (b) and in case of an attack on Availability, an attacker is able remove a message from the communication medium (c).*

1.2.1   Principles

The most basic concepts of security are commonly referred to as the CIA principles: Confidentiality (C), Integrity (I) and Availability (A) (see Figure 1.2). Some researchers also consider liability and anonymity, but these are not required in the automotive domain and thus will not be discussed here.

Confidentiality.   Confidentiality describes the protection against *reading* of messages by an attacker (see Figure 1.2(a)). Reading is generally possible whenever the communication medium is accessible to an attacker and messages are insufficiently or not at all encrypted. Thus, to ensure confidentiality, a sufficiently strong encryption method is required.

Integrity.   Integrity describes the protection against *creating* or *modifying* messages by an attacker (see Figure 1.2(b)). To protect the integrity of the message a Cipher-based Message Authentication Code (CMAC) is typically used. A CMAC is a Message Authentication Code (MAC) calculated based on the message itself and an encryption key. To avoid equal CMACs for equal messages, usually a random element is introduced, typically a unique random number (nonce). It is important to note that encryption does not guarantee integrity, as the message could be altered by an attacker, without the recipients being able to detect the change. In many communication systems, the attacker must not necessarily be able to read the message to be able to tamper with it.

Availability.   Availability describes the concept of an attacker not being able to *remove* messages from the communication system (see Figure 1.2(c)). This includes removal for all recipients (removal), as well as removal in a way such that the attacker himself can receive the message while intended recipients do not receive it (interrupt). Availability can not necessarily be ensured by additional measures taken on higher layers in the communication, but needs to be ensured by the communication system itself. Availability of a CAN message, e.g., can not be guaranteed, as any participant on the bus can alter the signal by sending a dominant bit at any time. If this alteration is performed while the message ID is transmitted and repeated for every retransmission of the message, the message is effectively removed from the bus.

1.2.2   Processes

To be able to guarantee the principles in the previous section, different processes are required. These will be explained in the following.

Encryption/Decryption.   Among the processes required for secure communication, the process of encrypting and decrypting messages is the most well-known. Encryption translates a plain text message into a cipher text message by means of a key. Depending on the type of encryption, this key might be secret (symmetric-key encryption) or publicly known (public-key encryption) (see Section 1.2.3). Decryption reverses the process and translates a cipher message into plain text, again by the use of a key. The decryption key is always secret.

Signing/Verifying.   When signing a message, a signature is added to the end of the message. The signature ensures that the sender of the message can be verified by the receivers and that the integrity property is fulfilled. To do so, the signature is typically based on the message itself, a unique random number (nonce) and the private key of the sender. To achieve the desired properties, public-key cryptography is used. As CMACs, based on symmetric-key cryptography, offer integrity, they are often considered signatures. However, they do not offer non-repudiation, meaning that the receivers can not verify who of the key holders sent a message. This is due to the fact that the same key is used for encryption and decryption and shared among all participants.

Authentication.   Authentication describes the process of securely identifying and validating a communication partner. Typically the authentication process is performed before any other communication processes are started. It is further used to exchange keys which are used in the following communication. This is typically achieved with public-key cryptography or a pre-programmed master key with symmetric-key cryptography (see Section 1.2.4).

Authorization.   Authorization is used to grant access to a resource. This is typically performed after communication participants are authenticated. Typically, a central control unit grants or revokes access to resources, configured through an Access Control List (ACL). Resources requested for authorization are, e.g., messages transmitted via the communication system, or overall access to the communication system.

1.2.3 Types of Cryptography

Cryptographic algorithms are usually distinguished in symmetric-key algorithms and public-key algorithms. These two types are explained in the following and depicted in Figure 1.3.

Symmetric-key Cryptography. In symmetric-key cryptography, a secret key is shared among the participants (see Figure 1.3(b)). Each of the participants can encrypt or decrypt messages with this key. To uphold the confidentiality of the communication, the key must be kept secret. It must thus be exchanged over a previously established secure channel between all participants. Symmetric-key cryptography can be implemented with relatively small resource requirements in software and, due to the typical repetitiveness of the algorithms, also be implemented more easily in hardware. Examples for symmetric-key algorithms are Advanced Encryption Standard (AES) [64, 120], Data Encryption Standard (DES) [117] and 3DES [64].

Public-key Cryptography. In public-key cryptography, two unique keys are required for every communication participant (see Figure 1.3(b)). One of these keys, the private key, is to be kept secret while the other, the public key, is publicly available to communication participants. The keys are mathematically dependent in a fashion that an encryption or decryption operation performed with one key, can only be reversed with the other key. Thus, a message encrypted with the public key can only be decrypted with the private key. This allows to send messages to the owner of the public key which can only be decrypted with his private key. Furthermore, public-key cryptography allows to sign messages with a private key and verify these with the public key. As the private key is secret, a corresponding message signature could have only been created by the holder of the key. Public-key algorithms are computationally intensive and limit the length of the clear text input. Thus, these algorithms are typically used to exchange symmetric keys, which are in turn used for communication. Examples for public-key cryptography algorithms are RSA [143] and Elliptic Curve Cryptography (ECC) [159].

1.2.4 Algorithms

After understanding the basics of cryptography and security, in this section, an overview over existing algorithms implementing and ensuring these concepts will be given. In the following, a quick overview over the advantages and disadvantages of algorithms is given. A countless number of algorithms have been developed throughout history. A full listing of algorithms is too extensive to be covered in this thesis. Thus, a short overview over the most widely used algorithms shall be given.

Data Protection Standard (DES). DES is a symmetric-key algorithm developed for the intelligence agencies in the United States of America (USA) in the 1970s [117]. It is now widely available in cryptographic software libraries and hardware implementations of cryptographic

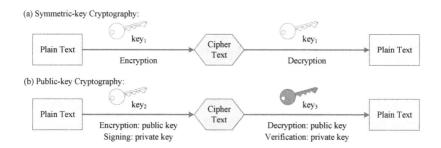

Figure 1.3: *Comparison of symmetric-key and public-key cryptography. In symmetri ckey cryptography, the keys for encryption and decryption are identical (key$_1$), in public-key cryptography two different keys (key$_2$, key$_3$) are used. This additionally allows signing and verification.*

accelerators. DES uses a key of length 56 Bits. This key size leads to insecurities, as with modern computer systems, a key can be determined by a brute force analysis (i.e. the testing of every possible key).

Triple DES (3DES). Triple DES has been developed to reuse the components of DES in 1998 [64]. It is based on DES, and in its main mode of operation is chaining three runs of the DES algorithm, each with a separate key of 56 Bits, thus increasing the key size to 168 Bits. It is currently considered secure. As DES has been designed for hardware support, software implementations of DES and Triple DES (3DES) are typically slower than comparable algorithms.

Advanced Encryption Standard (AES). The Advanced Encryption Standard (AES) is the National Institute of Standards and Technology (NIST) standard resulting from a cipher algorithm competition held by NIST and was announced in 2001 [64, 120]. It is a symmetric-key algorithm and the official successor to DES. AES can be used with keys of sizes 128 Bits, 192 Bits and 256 Bits. While attacks other than brute force have been shown, none of these attacks can be performed in reasonable time, with current computers the algorithm is thus considered secure. Today, AES is very commonly used, available in many software libraries, and as dedicated and integrated hardware accelerator.

RSA. RSA is a public-key algorithm widely used in many areas worldwide. It has first been presented in 1977 [143]. It exploits the difficulty of factorization of large numbers into two primes to achieve a secure relationship between public and private key. RSA is typically used with keys between 2048 and 4096 Bits. Keys of sizes lower than 1024 Bits can not be regarded as secure. While keys of 1024 Bits have not yet been broken in a practical use case, their use is discouraged [12]. RSA has a high computational complexity, resulting in long encryption and decryption times (see Chapter 4). Hardware accelerators are available, but integration of these with microcontrollers is less widespread than for AES.

Elliptic Curve Cryptography (ECC). ECC is a public-key algorithm that employs the difficulty of reversing a point multiplication of two points on an elliptic curve [159]. By not being able to reverse the multiplication, the asymmetry required for a public-key algorithm can be established. ECC is considered significantly more secure than RSA for equal key lengths. By being able to reduce the key length, the algorithm has the potential to execute significantly faster, as less operations are required. ECC is typically used with keys of size 256 Bits. While the concept of ECC has been proposed in 1985, the number of dedicated or integrated hardware accelerators is highly limited. There are, however, few software libraries available that support a subset of functions that fall under ECC, such as signing and verification.

1.2.5 Evaluating Security

With the large number of security algorithms and protocols, the question of comparability of these protocols is imminent. Evaluating security of algorithms and protocols for comparability is not trivial. In the following, a short overview over the evaluating of algorithms and security is given.

Symmetric Algorithms

Security algorithms are characterized by a number of factors and the internal structure is significantly different. This holds especially when comparing symmetric and public-key algorithms. The common denominator to all these algorithms is that a secret parameter, the cryptographic key is required. However, even the structure and functionality of keys can be significantly different. Thus, algorithms are typically only compared to algorithms of the same type (e.g. for symmetric vs public-key). For symmetric algorithms, the key lengths is one indicator for the strength of the algorithm. Furthermore, as in symmetric algorithms, the as the input is typically processed in blocks, the block length is a factor that can be compared. In the following, a short discussion on comparability based on the parameters key length and block size is given.

Key Length. The general assumption when comparing (established) cryptographic algorithms is that the algorithm in itself is secure. The security of the encrypted messages thus depends on the given parameters, these can be the key (and its length), as well as the clear text to be encrypted. The focus of security comparisons is thus on the key, and specifically its length. In case of the DES algorithm for example, the key length of 56 Bit is the weakest point in the system, allowing brute force attacks on encrypted messages. While a 56 Bit key length was still sufficient when the algorithm was developed, computers nowadays can process the amount of data much faster and thus find the key simply via trial and error of all combinations (brute force). To mitigate this attack and reuse the developed algorithm, 3DES was developed, using DES in three stages with three different keys, thus adding up security. While this is simplified and 3DES does not actually triple security, an increase in security is achieved. The discussion on key lengths also clearly shows the changing nature of security. As computational power is rising, following Moore's Law, larger keys or new algorithms are required to stay secure. In this fashion, DES was once considered secure, while today's computers can quickly brute force the relatively short key.

Block Size. Another issue when comparing algorithms is underlying block size and the handling of blocks. Blocks are the input on which algorithms operate. Longer clear text input needs to be cut to block size, shorter input needs to be padded. It is important to note that the block size determines the number of unique cipher blocks. Repetitions of blocks should be avoided, as they could enable an attacker to reverse engineer the key. The block size thus determines the maximum amount of data that can securely be encrypted. 3DES uses a block size of 64 Bits, limiting the amount of securely encryptable data with identical key to about 32 GB. AES, in turn uses 128 Bits, raising the amount of securely encryptable data by 2^{32}.

When encrypting data with such block based ciphers, it is important to note that when simply dividing clear text into blocks, identical clear text results in identical cipher text. This operating mode is called Electronic Code Block (ECB) and highly discouraged, as it can make patterns in the input easily identifiable. To avoid this, blocks should be combined or random factors be added. Other modes, such Cipher Block Chaining (CBC) or Cipher Feedback (CFB) perform such concatenation, and require a secure Initialization Vector (IV) as additional input. For these reasons, in this work, only AES in the CBC mode is used.

Asymmetric Algorithms

When comparing asymmetric algorithms, the internal workings of the algorithms lead to effects that key sizes alone can not be reasonable compared. For example, the RSA algorithm uses the difficulty of factorization of large numbers as the basis of security. ECC, in turn, uses the Elliptic Curve Discrete Logarithm Problem (ECDLP) as a basis. As these mathematical problems are fundamentally different, the comparison of parameters, such as key length, fails. ECC is considered more secure than RSA with identical key length. However, it is to note that this higher security strongly depends on the curve chosen for ECC, as the ECDLP can be solved efficiently for some curves [13, 160].

Protocols

In the security domain, protocols can be used to fulfill different tasks. Among these tasks are the exchange of keys, authentication and authorization. Similar to algorithms, the comparison of security of protocols is not trivial. While it is possible to show that a protocol can enforce the criteria envisioned, its security is based on the algorithms at the core of the protocol, thus referring back to the challenges above. Besides that, protocol concepts, just like algorithms, can be checked for flaws. Tools such as Scyther [18], allow to automate this analysis. An example for such an analysis is shown in Section 4.5.

Implementation

Although comparisons of algorithm and protocols are not trivial, it is possible to evaluate if they generally provide the level of security required for a project and chose an appropriate candidate. Yet, every week security problems are in the news all over the world. This is due to the fact that concepts might be secure, but their implementation might not be. While AES with the right key length is an excellent encryption algorithm, a library implementing AES could include a backdoor, sending the key to the developer of the library. In this case, although AES is secure, the library itself is not. Besides problems in configuration, this is the most common reason for security breaches on the Internet.

1.3   Automotive Security

Automotive communication systems and architectures have not been designed with security in mind. Traditionally, vehicles were separate entities without interconnections to other vehicles or networks. The communication systems in those vehicles have been designed for functionality and safety. Security was ensured by limiting access to the systems in the same fashion as access to the vehicle itself, through locked doors.

In recent years, the interconnectivity of devices, driven by the Internet of Things (IoT), has also reached the automotive domain [142]. Many vehicles are now connected to the Internet via cellular networks. Also networks between vehicles (car-to-car) and other devices (car-to-X) are proliferating at increasing speeds. Modern vehicles offer the integration of smartphones, either via WiFi or Bluetooth, enabling a further exchange of data. Today's vehicles can no longer be treated as isolated units in terms of network security, but need to be evaluated and designed as connected devices.

The OEMs, suppliers and also academia are reacting to these security challenges, but much effort is needed to secure vehicles appropriately. This is also due to the fact that the vehicle life cycle is relatively long for a device containing consumer electronic. The development time for a new vehicle generation is typically at least 3 years, while the lifetime of the vehicle on the road is upwards of 10 years [147]. Designing security measures to avoid attacks with the capabilities a future attacker will have over such a long time frame, is difficult.

1.3.1   External Security

Currently, the state of implementation of security in automotive systems is limited. While modern high-end vehicles often protect parts of their networks, these protection mechanisms are mostly at the perimeter of the vehicle networks, often manifesting as firewalls at gateways. With the increasing number of external connections, the attack surface rises. A number of attack vectors and the distance from which these can be exploited are shown in Figure 1.4.

To detect attacks, commercial Intrusion Detection Systems (IDSs) are available from suppliers [4, 170]. Connections to the Internet and cloud services are often (not always) protected with state-of-the-art security mechanisms at time of production. However, the support and upgrades of these systems, which is essential to keep protection mechanisms up-to-date, remains an open and fragmented issue. While some manufacturers include OTA update options, others require visits to an authorized workshop. Some manufacturers do not offer any updates.

Upcoming standards for vehicle-to-vehicle communications are expected to include authentication, authorization and encryption schemes, protecting the transmitted information. However, it is to note that the received information has a direct influence on the driving behavior of the vehicle and is thus highly sensitive. An attacker might, e.g., be able to influence following vehicles and force those to brake by altering the messages in his own vehicle, before those are transmitted via a secure connection. Sanity of vehicle-to-vehicle data will become increasingly important with the rising distribution and mandatory introduction of such systems. The mandatory introduction is expected in the USA from the year 2020 onwards [157]. The analysis of such security threats through external connections and the protection against are outside the scope of this thesis.

1.3.2   Internal Security

The protection mechanisms of in-vehicle networks are limited. While in the literature a multitude of mechanisms are proposed, so far the implementation of these systems in vehicles is minimal. A detailed overview over existing methods from both academia and industry is given in Section 1.6. While few exceptions exist, it is typically correct to say that no encryption is used for message transmissions on the internal networks for vehicles on the road today. Some manufacturers employ central gateways between different buses, allowing filtering of messages, which is often implemented in rudimentary rule-based systems. However, many manufacturers bridge buses directly, without further filters and some bypass their gateways with multi-bus ECUs, leading to security concerns. Judging the security of networks in general is not trivial and no general statement can be made. This thesis seeks to improve this (see Chapter 3).

The properties of the predominant vehicle communication system CAN make implementation of security difficult (see Section 1.1.3). The limited data rate, limited amount of data per message and the lack of secure sender and receiver identification make CAN a difficult basis for security. As a short message size allows only a very limited amount of different messages, an attacker can more easily reverse the encryption, making a meaningful encryption impossible. The low data rate of CAN makes transmissions of large messages, e.g., for certificates in authentication processes, impossible. While the data rate is higher in other systems such as FlexRay, the rigid structure and limited amount of bytes per message remain a challenge.

However, the increasing data rate requirements in vehicles today, having to support camera and radar sensors, among others, are triggering a redesign of the networks in all major vehicle manufacturers. The networks in next generation upper class vehicles will likely be based on Ethernet, providing a sufficient bandwidth and more reliable, though not inherently secure, identification of communication partners. As Ethernet also requires point-to-point connections, a fundamentally different topology compared to the CAN bus structure, a redesign of the complete network architecture is required. This major redesign is a chance for the vehicle manufacturers to incorporate security considerations and best practices into the network architecture.

1.3.3   Device Security

Another aspect of security in vehicles is the security of the ECUs, gateways and other devices. Here, one can differentiate between software and hardware security. Increasingly, ECUs are equipped with cryptographic accelerators and secure memory, allowing higher standards of security. This includes password protected and sometimes signed ECU updates and, in some cases, strategies for secure boot. However, these protection mechanisms are often insufficient and have been circumvented. The tuning community makes use of such exploits in a large scale, with e.g., through chip-tuning.

The aspects of device security are not only of significant importance for the customer, but also for the manufacturer. Chip-tuning and product piracy are important factors, potentially leading to financial losses for the manufacturer. Chip-tuning may additionally raise questions of liability. If an unauthorized software is installed on an ECU, the manufacturer does not have to assume liability for malfunctions. However, proving the installation of such software is not trivial. Thus, manufacturers are working on improved protection mechanisms for software and hardware of devices. Here, Physically Unclonable Functions (PUFs) are becoming increasingly important [162].

1.3.4   Standardization

Standards addressing security exist in different domains. Starting from a high-level organizational perspective, ISO/IEC 27001 [74] and ISO/IEC 27002 [75] outline requirements for Information Security Management Systems (ISMSs) in organizations and for individuals handling these, respectively. To evaluate and certify the security of systems, typically the "Common Criteria" are used. These are specified in ISO/IEC 15408 parts 1-3 [63, 60, 61]. More specifically the embedded and real-time systems domain is addressed in the ISA/IEC 62443 series of standards. Starting from part 1-1 [47] to part 3-3 [48], it provides guidance for security through the complete life cycle and all components in Industrial Automation and Control Systems (IACS).

While the above standards can in part be applied to the automotive domain, the underlying concepts are also integrated into automotive standards. Not directly relating to security but a core standard of safety and thus heavily influenced by security issues is ISO 26262, parts 1-10 ([67] to [68]). First security considerations for the automotive domain have been laid out in SAE J3061 [144]. There, existing approaches from other domains have been applied as guidelines and best practices to the automotive industry. Furthermore, AUTOSAR specifies to use security for message transmissions in its version 4.2.2. There, high-level abstractions for the Secure Onboard Communication (SecOC) module, such as the use of Message Authentication Codes (MACs) for authentication of senders and messages are proposed [7, 9]. AUTOSAR uses symmetric keys. An Application Programming Interface (API) for cryptographic operations, such as encryption and decryption, but also key exchange, is defined in the specification of the Crypto Abstraction Library (CAL) [8]. It is important to note that these definitions are an abstract API and no algorithms or protocols for implementation are defined here. Thus any developed framework can be integrated with the AUTOSAR specification by fulfilling the API requirements. Furthermore, [9] clearly states "The SecOC module has not been specified to work with MOST and LIN communication networks. With MOST not being specifically supported, the applicability to multimedia and telematic car domains may be limited.". Considering the high risk of attacks through telematics and the infotainment domain, this is a significant gap.

1.3.5 Legal Situation

Of high importance in the domain of automotive security is the legal framework. A complete survey of the worldwide legal situation exceeds this thesis, but a short overview shall be given. While legislation exists for the safety of vehicles, as well as their operation and service, security is not yet addressed by existing laws. In many countries, bills concerning vehicle security have been proposed and are under discussion in local parliaments at time of writing (e.g., [33, 100]). These bills can be divided into the categories security and privacy.

On the one hand, these bills seek to secure the vehicles, their external and internal connections, as described in Sections 1.3.1 and 1.3.2, respectively. On the other hand, the highly digitized vehicles of today generate large amounts of data, ranging from navigational information over speed, acceleration and braking information to speech recorded via the internal microphones, e.g., for voice calls. The current legal situation is unclear about the ownership of this data. Vehicle owners can not access or delete this data, also in case their vehicle is sold. In many cases, such data is transmitted to the manufacturer for analysis [101]. Currently, no law governs the treatment and ownership of such data, resulting in privacy concerns.

Though not directly addressing security, some legacy legislation with impact on security exists. One example of such legislation interfering with current security concerns is the requirement of the OBD port. The requirements for this diagnostics port are following the principles in competition law, requiring a possibility also for manufacturer independent workshop to diagnose and service the vehicle. Its requirements are laid out in the laws of a number of countries (e.g., [29, 31]) and includes the specification of a communication protocol which does not offer encryption or authorization. With such requirements by law, securing all in-vehicle traffic is difficult. A weak link will remain in the form of the diagnostics port.

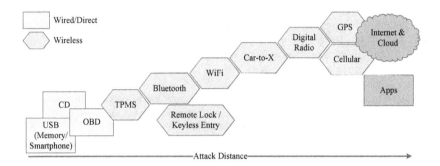

Figure 1.4: *Attack paths into the vehicle and distance required for attack. Direct access is needed for media, such as USB smartphone connectors and CDs, and the On-Board Diagnostics (OBD) port. Wireless access can be possible via short range systems, such as the Tire Pressure Monitor System (TPMS) or long distance, such as by overriding the Global Positioning System (GPS) signal. Apps installed on the infotainment system are a special case, as these are distributed over the Internet, but installed locally.*

This section shall only serve as a short introduction into the complicated legal situation around security in cars. The remainder of this thesis focuses on technical approaches to automotive security.

1.3.6 Attack Examples

In the following, a few examples of automotive security and attacks on the same shall be discussed. These descriptions will focus on digital attacks, resulting from the increased interconnectivity and digitization of cars and will not further discuss conventional lock picking mechanisms. The examples mentioned here can be broadly divided into three categories. In the first category, all attacks resulting in the opening of the vehicle doors are summarized. The second category describes attacks on the internal vehicle networks, where an attacker has local access to the vehicle (local attacks). Finally, the third category summarizes all attacks on the internal vehicle networks, where an attacker does not require local access (remote attacks).

Accessing of the vehicle.   The first category is an essential basis for many attacks in the local access category. The access to the internal vehicle networks is significantly easier when access to the vehicle is obtained. In that case, the diagnostics port can be used for further network access. Multiple different attacks demonstrated in laboratory situations and observed by the police in the wild fall into this category. The obvious attacks are standard lock picking or the smashing of windows. Protection against these mechanical attacks are outside the scope of this thesis and will not be further discussed here. Picking of the digital locks, i.e. the remote lock opening/closing function also falls in this category. Here, different attacks have been demonstrated. These range from simple brute-force code guessing devices, emulating the remote control of the driver over the sophisticated reverse engineering of vehicle remote security chips [175] to attacks on connections to smartphone vehicle apps [80, 1] and "Keyless Entry" systems [36]. Once having gained access to the car, an attacker might steal any of the contents of the vehicle or use the OBD port to access the internal vehicle networks for further damage. Note that it is in most cases not directly possible to drive the car, as the immobilizer is typically still blocking the starting of the motor.

Local attacks.   With access to the inside of the vehicle and specifically the diagnosis port, an attacker can proceed with attacks from the second category. Here, all attacks are summarized which are directly executed over a wired connection to the vehicle. Typically, such a connection is established via a CAN or OBD to Universal Serial Bus (USB) adapter. Such adapters allow to receive and transmit messages from and to the internal networks, which, in case not further shielded by a gateway, are fully accessible to an attacker. With a successful connection to the internal network, an attacker generally has the same possibilities as the owner and authorized workshop personal. However, vehicles differ significantly and large amounts of reconnaissance work might be necessary to execute all functions. Furthermore, messages might be filtered by a central gateway and the attacker might not be able to send any message freely to any recipient. Bypassing the gateway manually and connecting to the target bus circumvents this protection mechanism. The attacker can potentially also read and reprogram the software on ECUs in the network. However, some vehicle elements, such as central ECUs, e.g., the engine control unit or the immobilizer might further be protected against reprogramming, e.g. by passwords. Attacks in this category have been presented in the literature. Typically, these attacks have been performed under laboratory conditions [85, 15, 105]. Additionally, a large number of services exist worldwide, using exploits in this category to alter the mileage counter of vehicles, reprogram keys and bypass immobilizers, e.g., to add a "Start Engine" button. Many of these services are illegal, yet devices to perform such access are easily available online [28, 156].

Remote attacks.   Another access mode entirely is the third category of remote access. Here, the attacker tries to access the vehicle via remote connections, such as a cellular Internet connection. This includes the challenge of first identifying the vehicle on the Internet, before executing the attack first on the gateway device and in the following on the internal networks of the vehicle. The feasibility of such attacks has been presented under laboratory conditions in [15] and [107]. A significant amount of reconnaissance about the vehicle to be attacked is required here. However, with increased standardization of the vehicle Internet gateways, such as the infotainment system with apps in Google's Android Auto [37] and Apple's CarPlay [3], the hurdles for this access method will decrease. Similar to malicious apps on smartphones, an attacker might deceive the user to install a malicious app for his vehicle, bypassing the gateway protection mechanisms entirely.

Another aspect of remote attacks is the misuse of protective systems. In 2010, reports described the misuse of a system in Austin, Texas, USA meant to track and disable vehicles of clients not paying installments for their vehicle loans [134]. In this case, a laid off employee disabled the engines of more than 100 vehicles, while at the same time activating their horns. The employee used a former colleagues account to access the web-based system. While from a technical perspective this was a legitimate action that is hard to prevent, clearly such situations pose high inconvenience to the vehicle user and should not happen. This illustrates the influence of societal aspects on vehicle security.

An additional threat might result from actions of the owner of the vehicle. While the owner himself is typically considered trustworthy, he does have access to the OBD port. In recent years, multiple OBD dongles have appeared in the market, promising diagnosis and tuning functions via this port. Furthermore, some vehicle insurance providers offer discounts for good driving behavior. Typically, this is achieved by tracking the speed, mileage and location via an OBD adapter [104, 135]. Some of these adapters are equipped with Bluetooth connections to connect to the owners smartphone [6], others have built-in cellular modems, effectively bridging the internal vehicles networks to the Internet [185]. In case these devices are not secure, attackers can take over these devices and execute any function, as if directly connected to the OBD port. Such attacks have been presented in the literature [34, 125, 166]. While the owner is not the attacker in this scenario, he certainly is a threat.

Disclosure policies. In software companies it is common practice to operate vulnerability disclosure programs and even to offer bounties for vulnerabilities reported. These programs are used to attract freelance security researchers to spend time with the products of a company and test them for security. In turn for the bounty, the security researcher hands over all data collected about a vulnerability before releasing it in public, which allows the company to fix it before any damage to its customers. This process is not yet common practice in the automotive domain. First companies are experimenting with such programs [14, 40], but their introduction is not yet widespread. This makes it difficult for security researchers and the public to get into contact with a manufacturer, in case a security flaw is found in its cars.

1.3.7 Summary

This short overview over the state of automotive security reveals a large number of challenges across all sectors. Starting from the in-vehicle communications, over external connections and vehicle locks all the way to legal frameworks. These challenges are not all of technical, but also societal nature, requiring new approaches. In this thesis, some of the technical approaches shall be addressed. Challenges for these are outlined in the following section.

1.4 Challenges

After the basic understanding of automotive communication systems, as well as security systems, as they are implemented in consumer networks today, this section will focus on the challenges existing when combining these two domains. Multiple challenges need to be overcome. The complexity and heterogeneity of automotive networks create challenges at design time, as well as runtime. In the following, some of the technical challenges will be explored.

1.4.1 Design Time

Managing the complexity of security in automotive networks through all phases of the life cycle is critical. This includes the design time at the start of the life cycle.

Analysis. It is important to understand and evaluate the security of the complete architecture, as this enables comparisons of different architectures and is the basis for informed decisions on security. It is possible to analyze single devices and their hardware and software components for security, e.g., through evaluation frameworks and expert audits. However, the size and complexity of complete automotive architectures complicates the analysis. While other networks, such as the Internet, are larger and more complex, these are typically not analyzed as a whole. Due to the prevalent architectures in the automotive domain, however, there are no gateways fully separating the network. Thus, the architecture as a whole needs to be analyzed to characterize all influences.

Another factor to be considered at design time is the lifetime of the vehicle. As vehicles are typically on the road for ten years and longer, the security decisions made at design time have to hold up throughout the years the car is on the road [147]. The computational capabilities of attackers, however, develop significantly within this time. Furthermore, security flaws and attack possibilities might be discovered while the car is on the road. This development over time needs to be taken into account while designing the in-vehicle architecture. While some of these new flaws might be fixed through software patches by the manufacturer, flaws in the hardware design can not be rectified easily. For issues, such as changing the bus an ECU is connected to, an expensive recall would be required. Furthermore, one can assume that, similar to the consumer electronics domain, software patches will not be supplied indefinitely.

Currently, no evaluation frameworks for the security of in-vehicle networks exists. No standards have been established and no best practices have been formulated.

Synthesis. Adjacent domains, such as the safety of vehicles, already heavily rely on modeling and verification techniques to analyze and verify the safety of vehicle designs. Furthermore, these verification approaches have been extended to synthesis, allowing to synthesize new safe systems from a set of requirements and models of the subsystems. Similarly, security analysis can form the basis of a model-based security synthesis. This synthesis can generate architectures or subsystems based on the security requirements defined for functions, subsystems and the overall architecture. An exhaustive search can be performed with the above analysis as feedback. This way, the most secure architecture or subsystem for a given set of requirements can be synthesized based on the values determined by the analysis.

To accommodate all safety and security requirements in the synthesis process, future systems will likely need to take an integrated approach. In this approach, safety and security need to be considered, based on their respective modeling and verification approaches and a combined synthesis is required. Only such an integrated model-based safety and security synthesis can ensure that complex future architectures are safe and secure. As currently no analysis frameworks exist and these form the basis for model-based synthesis, no synthesis approach exists.

1.4.2   Runtime

While design time analysis helps determining the fixed structure of the architecture, it is required to ensure security at runtime as well. This includes the security of messages and ECU software, as well as ensuring that only legitimate communication participants transmit legitimate messages, and that all participants can be identified. Ensuring these security criteria is challenging in automotive networks and causes a lot of challenges. These can be broadly summarized into the categories *Latency*, *Bandwidth* and *Computation and Storage*. In the following, these challenges are shortly described.

Latency. As automotive communication systems implement distributed control systems required for the safety of the vehicle, these systems follow the real-time requirements laid out in Section 1.1.1. Automotive communication systems need to respond within a range of 1 to 10 milliseconds, for some systems in the range of microseconds. Retransmissions of messages are generally not possible. On the other hand, fulfilling security requirements usually requires a certain amount of time in itself, depending on the chosen algorithm and protocol. Using a software implementation on an embedded processor with limited computational capability can drive the required time for encryption and decryption into the area of 1 to 30 seconds or even higher. This holds especially for asymmetric cryptography, such as required in authentication and key exchange protocols. Implementing such protocols in the automotive domain is challenging and consequently most existing protocols use a pre-shared key leading to a decrease of security.

These requirements seem to be contradicting. In this thesis, we will show that this contradiction can be resolved by optimizing the authentication protocol for the use in automotive contexts. By using domain knowledge, such as the detailed construction and operation of communication systems and security protocols in vehicles, latencies can be reduced significantly.

Bandwidth. Similar to the latency requirements, the bandwidth requirements of security protocols versus the bandwidth capabilities of automotive communication systems are highly divergent. While upcoming automotive communication systems on the upper end of the bandwidth range support similar speeds to consumer networks (10 to 100 MBit/s), widespread legacy communication systems and other networks designed for time-critical control data do not provide sufficient bandwidth (125 kBit/s to 1 MBit/s) to shoulder the additional requirements of security protocols. The protocols used in corporate networks and the Internet are used with connection speeds that are typically in the range of 1 MBit/s to 1 GBit/s. This is also visible in the amount of data per packet, which is often the largest unit that can be transmitted on the bus, as segmentation is typically not specified in the automotive domain. The amount of data per packet in vehicles is too short to implement a meaningful encryption, which cannot easily be broken by brute force attacks, let alone an authentication protocol. Typical message content lengths are in the range of 8 to 40 Bytes. By contrast, Ethernet offers packet sizes of up to 1500 Bytes.

Again, the requirements of security and the automotive domain seem contradictory. However, by extending the existing standards, this thesis will demonstrate that secure messaging is possible, also on low bandwidth networks.

Computation and Storage. The ECUs used in automotive settings are of varying computational power and storage. While some devices, such as the engine control unit or the infotainment unit have a rather large amount of computational power and storage, most ECUs are much smaller, having slower processors and little memory. Current infotainment units are typically using single- or multi-core CPUs with frequencies in the range of hundreds of Megahertz or even Gigahertz and multiple Gigabytes of Random Access Memory (RAM), as well as dedicated GPUs, similar to the processors in modern smartphones and tablets [123, 137, 121]. Compared to that, slower ECUs, such as for user input switches are 8-Bit processors with frequencies in the range of 20-40 Mhz and typically below 8 kB of RAM [122, 138]. However, security mechanisms as those shown above require complex computations, especially in case of asymmetric cryptography. This further challenges the implementation of effective security in the automotive domain.

As shown in this thesis, security can be achieved by selecting the parameters of the security algorithms and protocols carefully and by optimizing protocols for the use in environments of low computational power.

1.5   Contributions

This thesis proposes three approaches for analyzing and securing in-vehicle E/E architectures. These approaches target both the design time and runtime aspects of security. Specifically proposed are (1) a design time analysis for security in automotive networks, (2) a lightweight authentication framework for authentication and authorization in automotive networks, and (3) a flexible message transmission scheme demonstrated on FlexRay, extending message sizes and thus enabling security measures on time-triggered communication systems. These main contributions are detailed in the following.

Security Analysis for Automotive Networks (SAAN).   The basis for informed decisions in any domain is the knowledge of the system. Decisions and comparisons regarding security are difficult, as it is not trivial to quantify security. Typically, security evaluations are used, which are based on expert analysis, supported by security analysis frameworks. These evaluations are applied for hardware and software components. Currently, there is no option to analyze complete automotive architectures or subsystems inside an architecture for security. This analysis, however, is important, as the security of functions is heavily influenced by the architecture these functions are implemented in.

This thesis proposes the Security Analysis for Automotive Networks (SAAN), which provides a method to analyze messages and functions in automotive architectures for security. The analysis is based on the network architecture and established methods for component evaluation. The architecture contains all devices, such as ECUs and gateways, interconnections between devices, and messages transmitted by these devices. The component evaluation describes the exploitability and patchability of devices. Exploitability and patchability describe how fast new security vulnerabilities, e.g. buffer overflows in the telematics unit [15], are discovered and how fast these can be fixed, e.g. via software updates, respectively. While exploitability depends highly on the design of the device, patchability depends mostly on the software update cycle. These rates reasonably approximate the behavior of the system by defining the maximum time between two exploits/patches.

To take into account the rates for exploitability and patchability, so the probabilities and time-dependency of the system, a probabilistic model checking approach is used. As times might vary in reality and exploitability and patching rates are not fixed, such variations are accounted for in the model checking algorithm as exponential distributions for the occurrence probabilities. To represent the time basis and probabilities of the evaluation, this thesis proposes an efficient Continuous-Time Markov Chain (CTMC) model synthesis from the automotive architecture and component evaluation, allowing model checking of the system [86].

State-space reduction and speed up of the computation are achieved by taking into account the behavior and dependencies of typical automotive networks in the model generation. These dependencies are flexibly defined as rules for every component. A CAN bus is, e.g., always exploitable in terms of availability, i.e. susceptible to overriding of messages, as soon as one of the attached ECUs is exploitable.

In addition to the model, a property needs to be defined, specifying the element or combination of elements of the architecture to be analyzed, as well as the time frame for analysis. The CTMC and the property are then analyzed with probabilistic model checking algorithms from literature [87]. The results describe the exploitability of the element to be analyzed within the given time frame. E.g., an ECU can be analyzed for how long it is exploitable via a given bus within one year.

SAAN is evaluated on different architectures to prove its capabilities to find security flaws. By enabling an evaluation of security in automotive networks, comparisons between different architectures are possible. Through the automotive-specific model generation, the model size is decreased by five orders of magnitude, in turn improving model checking performance by two to three orders of magnitude over state of the art model generation.

Lightweight Authentication for Secure Automotive Networks (LASAN). The second approach is focused on securing in-vehicle network traffic. Meeting the real-time requirements of automotive networks means that the secure setup needs to be performed efficiently. To secure traffic, it is required to encrypt messages, authenticate communication participants and authorize messages. This is typically ensured by authentication frameworks.

Traditional authentication frameworks, such as Transport Layer Security (TLS) [23] or Kerberos [119, 184], however, have high requirements for computation and data rate, which are incompatible with automotive systems. These frameworks are employed in corporate networks or the Internet, where real-time requirements are lower and high data rates for message transmissions are available. Asymmetric cryptography is used in the establishment of message streams.

This thesis proposes Lightweight Authentication for Secure Automotive Networks (LASAN). LASAN is specifically tuned to the automotive environment by providing authentication for ECUs against a central root of trust, the security module. Authentication is performed in an asynchronous fashion, thus not interfering with real-time requirements. Authenticated ECUs may request authorization of message streams, which is granted based on manufacturer defined Access Control Lists (ACL). Authorization is fully based on symmetric cryptography, minimizing the required time, and can be performed as required, or upfront at the start of the vehicle to minimize the influence on real-time message transmissions further. A successful authorization also contains a symmetric message key, allowing to encrypt the following data message symmetrically.

Evaluations show that LASAN allows to set up message streams two to three orders of magnitude faster than the state of the art. As LASAN has been optimized for the automotive domain, it can be easily integrated with and support existing automotive processes, such as Over-The-Air (OTA) updates or workshop maintenance and repair.

Policy-based scheduling using FlexRay. Implementing security on legacy communications systems is challenging. Authentication and authorization, e.g., require to transmit relatively large amounts of data in a short amount of time, but typically do not require periodical transmissions. This is difficult to implement on time-triggered communication systems. Furthermore, to ensure secure communication, a minimum amount of entropy must be available per message, if multiple similar or equal messages are sent. This means that messages can not be too short in size, as otherwise brute force attacks on encrypted messages become possible.

Existing time-triggered communication systems, such as FlexRay, are highly limited in their flexibility regarding message lengths and transmission times, limiting the entropy available for security. FlexRay is a time-triggered communication system with data rates of up to 10 MBit/s allowing to guarantee message transmission times [70]. It is thus highly suitable for safety-critical data transmissions. However, the schedule for all message transmissions needs to be defined at design time and cannot be changed at runtime. The policy-based scheduling for FlexRay presented in this thesis enables a higher flexibility for messages on the bus. Assignments of timeslots are treated more flexible, and slots are assigned to ECUs, which in turn place messages based on a pre-defined policy. Thus, a virtual communication layer is established, allowing to utilize the combined timeslots for message transmissions. Timeslot lengths do not limit message lengths in such a systems, and short bursts or message transmissions, such as generated by authentication frameworks can be handled. Furthermore, as the underlying FlexRay system does not need to be changed, full compatibility to existing FlexRay implementations is kept.

Evaluating the proposed scheduling shows a decrease in message transmission latencies by close to one order of magnitude over conventional FlexRay scheduling. Additionally, message sizes and periods can be selected freely and are no longer bound to the restrictions set by the communication system.

The rise of interconnectivity in vehicles raises many challenges in the domain of security. The seemingly contrary requirements of security and real-time are analyzed and solved in this thesis for three specific challenges. While the contributions are set in the context of the automotive domain, they are, with generalization, applicable to other domains with similar requirements, as well. As such, this thesis contributes to the combination of security and real-time requirements beyond the scope of the automotive domain.

1.6 Related Work

The following is an overview over the general literature in the area of automotive security, including threats, countermeasures and integration. Additionally, adjacent domains to the automotive application are explored. Literature directly related to the individual contributions will be discussed in the respective chapters.

1.6.1 Automotive Threats

Currently, most internal communication in vehicles is insecure. Encryption is rare, and, if available, often uses similar keys across a series of vehicles and ECUs. Authentication is used especially when reprogramming ECUs, conventional data transmissions are typically not encrypted or authenticated. The first extensive overviews of security in modern networked vehicles were presented in [85] and [15], where it was shown that ECUs could be attacked and reprogrammed directly, by obtaining pre-programmed security keys from the car tuning community. Most of these attacks have been performed with direct connections to the vehicle, but in [15] attacks via external interfaces such as the integrated telematics unit have also been reported. More recently, in [105], two vehicles were attacked extensively and in [106], multiple other vehicles were qualitatively analyzed. The attacks by [105] were executed over direct connections to vehicles, either to the OBD port or the networks directly. In [107], these attacks have been extended and performed via a cellular connection. Further examples for attacks specifically for the CAN network and countermeasures have been presented in [46]. A case study investigating the likelihood of attacks on vehicles based on expert knowledge has been presented in [11].

To access the inside of the vehicle for further attacks, the locking system needs to be circumvented. In the literature, different analyses of locking systems and their attack vectors have been presented. In [36], signals of keyless entry systems have been relayed over longer distances, allowing to open vehicles without the key fob being present at the vehicle. Furthermore, smartphone apps by vehicle manufacturers have been analyzed in the literature. Some of these apps offer the opening of the car from distance and can be circumvented [80]. Once in the vehicle, the OBD port and vehicle networks can be accessed for further attacks. To start the motor, the immobilizer needs to be bypassed. An attack on immobilizer chips has been presented in [175]. Many of the presented attacks are limited to a certain make and model of a vehicle. Often, such specific attacks are not found by researchers and published, but are available in the tuning and car theft communities online.

1.6.2 Intrusion Detection, Network Analysis & Verification

Intrusion Detection systems are commonly used in corporate networks to discover attacks in the network, e.g., based on known message patterns for attacks or continuous comparison of traffic to a baseline [21]. In [106], a vehicle IDS has been proposed to detect anomalies in the vehicle network traffic by constantly comparing traffic to a baseline. The approach in [45] utilizes concepts like detection models known from the computer domain and ports these to the automotive domain. There, also the interaction with the driver is investigated, as responses from IDSs in a safety-critical context can not always be automated. Other approaches, such as [116] are based on the entropy of traffic, allowing a flexible detection of attacks without requiring predefined attack patterns. Intrusion detection can be significantly more difficult when attackers do not perform their attacks in a straight forward fashion, but instead try to hide their intentions by obfuscating their attacks. In [25], a method to detect obfuscated attacks is described. Commercial IDSs are available, but their inner workings are not publicly available [4, 170].

To validate the security of in-vehicle networks, [158] propose a combined evaluation of safety and security requirements of an AUTomotive Open System ARchitecture (AUTOSAR) architecture.

1.6.3   Encryption and Hardware Support

Initial efforts to introduce encryption into real-time vehicular networks have been presented in the literature [145]. To unify protection efforts, the Hersteller Initiative Software (HIS) has specified a cryptographic accelerator, called Secure Hardware Extension (SHE) for use in vehicles [30]. The SHE is a cryptographic accelerator with cryptographic storage and is based on the security module defined as EVITA Hardware Security Module (HSM) light in the EVITA project [152]. Support for encryption and key storage can also be achieved with a Trusted Platform Module (TPM) [62]. Microcontrollers used in ECUs are in many cases available with integrated compatible hardware security modules [123, 5]. In [153], security functions are integrated into the hardware of the network controller, achieving higher real-time performance and determinism than layered approaches. Similarly, [154] proposes a seamless integration of security on system-level, based on FPGA reconfiguration techniques.

To limit the latency impact on the real-time communication, symmetric cryptography such as AES [120] and the AES-based CMAC [26] have been chosen in the SHE and elsewhere in the literature, since these approaches are computationally simpler. These algorithms are significantly faster, especially with the hardware support of the SHE. Symmetric encryption requires that secret keys are known to all participants of a protected communication. This opens a new attack vector, as keys are often pre-programmed into ECUs and valid for the lifetime of the ECU [85]. In case a key becomes known, such as described in [85], attacks for the lifetime of vehicles or possibly on complete vehicle fleets are possible. These scaling effects can be dangerous, as an attacker can leverage an attack on millions of vehicles. With the more widespread use of vehicles in external networks, this recovery and publishing of secret keys will increase, as more groups can reap the benefits. An approach to mitigate scaling effects through obfuscation of CAN message IDs has been proposed in [97].

1.6.4   Security Integration

One approach to employing symmetric cryptography and limiting the overhead of additional security in legacy communication systems is to use Message Authentication Codes (MACs). These are based on symmetric cryptography, allowing fast and efficient computation, especially on ECUs with limited computational power. In [94], MACs are introduced to CAN and safety and security are considered in an integrated functional model mapped to a CAN architecture. In [42], an approach to introduce MACs into FlexRay is presented. There, the Timed Efficient Stream Loss-Tolerant Authentication (TESLA) protocol is employed for time-delayed release of keys in the time-triggered segment of FlexRay. While TESLA supports sender authentication with symmetric mechanisms, it does not authenticate communication partners or authorize communication streams. In [180], a CMAC is utilized and integrated with the CRC of the underlying communication system, reducing the overhead and achieving the required sender authentication and message integrity checks. By including the security considerations in the design phase of systems, [79] achieve time efficiency with low hardware overhead. To be able to ensure real-time behavior, all of these approaches employ symmetric cryptography, requiring a pre-shared key.

Others, such as [44] propose the use of Virtual CANs (VCANs), similar to virtual networks in the consumer and corporate domains, to separate network traffic.

1.6.5 Other domains

While the above approaches focus on in-vehicle networks, the adjacent domain of car-to-x (car-2-x, c2x) technologies received more extensive coverage in literature. Noteworthy here is the Secure Vehicle Communication (SeVeCom) project [81]. This outlined a first attacker model and proposed security mechanisms for c2x networks. SeVeCom proposes to rely on multiple levels (long-term, short-term) of public-key mechanisms. This approach has been used in other projects and multiple consortia are now working on c2x technologies. However, participants need sufficient computational resources for asymmetric cryptography to implement these systems. These resources are typically available for selected ECUs communicating with external vehicles, such as in the c2x scenario, but not necessarily for every ECU in the vehicle.

Significant progress in securing communication has been achieved in other areas where embedded systems are used to transmit data. The smart grid is a prime example of progress in this domain. Multiple approaches have been described in literature to achieve this. In [132] a system-level approach to secure smart meters has been proposed, based on the hardware support presented in [131]. In [155] an approach to secure communication for the smart grid has been proposed. There, TLS has been used to secure the communication of the backbone. However, in comparison to smart metering applications, the real-time constraints in the automotive domain are far stricter.

1.6.6 Summary

The above overview of existing literature given here is a general introduction to automotive security and adjacent areas. More detailed work relating directly to the contributions of this thesis will be discussed in the individual chapters. There, also the differentiation of the individual approaches will be discussed in greater detail.

The contributions in this thesis seek to prevent some of the automotive threats discussed in Section 1.6.1. Note that the prevention methods presented in this thesis focus on attacks executed in the internal vehicle network. Methods to prevent external entry, e.g., a firewall at the telematics unit, will not be discussed. All attack scenarios in this thesis assume that an attacker already has access to the internal vehicle networks. However, the impact of attacks through external interfaces on the internal systems is considered in Chapter 3.

The contributions in this thesis complement other defense techniques, such as Intrusion Detection (IDS) and Prevention Systems (IPS). While IDS and IPS seek to detect and prevent ongoing malicious actions by an attacker with access to the internal network, the proposed authentication framework in this thesis seeks to prevent such access beforehand. In case this should fail for any reason, an IDS or IPS comes into play to take additional actions, limiting the attacker's options.

Existing evaluation methods for vehicle security, such as [158], evaluate systems based on Hardware-in-the-loop (HIL) and Software-in-the-loop (SIL) tests. To perform these tests, the systems or the respective parts under test need to be developed and built. Security Analysis for Automotive Networks (SAAN), as presented in Chapter 3, complements such evaluation systems and does not show this restriction. Vehicle systems and concepts can be analyzed without the need to built a prototype of the system. This allows to judge the security of a system early in the development process. As SAAN verifies concepts, this does not necessarily replace HIL and SIL analysis required to identify implementation flaws.

The cryptographic approaches presented in literature form the basis of the contributions in this thesis. Developing secure and efficient cryptographic algorithms is a highly complex mathematical matter. Therefore, proven algorithms and encryption schemes should be used in applications. We follow these recommendations and built on existing work. Similarly, we utilize cryptographic accelerators to speed up encryption and decryption processes. More details and comparisons will be presented in Chapter 4.

In a similar fashion, the proposed approaches can make use of integration as shown in Section 1.6.4. Integration with MACs can minimize the required bandwidth further. Such optimizations of the proposed approaches are highly dependent on the utilized bus systems, but should be considered in future work. An approach for integrating security into FlexRay is proposed in Chapter 5. Other approaches, such as VCANs [44], are orthogonal to the proposed approaches can be used to complement these.

In summary, the contributions of this thesis are utilizing some of the existing concepts and can complement others to achieve security for automotive E/E architectures.

1.7 Organization and Bibliographic Notes

This work has been performed under the Campus for Research Excellence And Technological Enterprise (CREATE) program and was financially supported by the Singapore National Research Foundation (NRF). Within the CREATE program, Technische Universität München (TUM) CREATE focuses on electric vehicles. One of the goals of TUM CREATE was the development of an electric taxi. The developed taxi EVA and specifically its infotainment system will be introduced in Chapter 2. In the development of this infotainment system, a number of security challenges surfaced. These security challenges significantly influenced the remaining chapters of this thesis. We thus motivate the contributions of this thesis through the design experience gained with EVA, as detailed in Chapter 2. Parts of this have been published in [128].

In Chapter 3, the focus is on the security of the overall communication system, including all its components and interfaces. There, an approach to evaluate architecture security at design time with probabilistic model checking is described. Parts of this work have been published in [115].

Chapter 4 uses the design example shown in Chapter 2 to design a secure authentication framework for the use in the automotive domain. This framework permits authentication and authorization at runtime, is verified for security, and integrated with the automotive lifecycle. Furthermore, a simulator for the evaluation of security in automotive networks is proposed. Parts of this work have been published in [111], [112] and [114].

As the requirements for the approaches in Chapter 4 are not necessarily given in legacy communication systems, Chapter 5 introduces a method to utilize the existing communication system FlexRay more flexibly while keeping all guarantees. Parts of this work have been published in [113].

Parts of this thesis are available in the following publications:

- Philipp Mundhenk, Andrew Paverd, Artur Mrowca, Sebastian Steinhorst, Martin Lukasiewycz, Suhaib A. Fahmy, Samarjit Chakraborty. **Security in Automotive Networks: Lightweight Authentication and Authorization**. In: ACM Transactions on Design Automation of Electronic Systems (TODAES) 22, 2 (2017), pp. 25:1–25:27. DOI: 10.1145/2960407

- Philipp Mundhenk, Artur Mrowca, Sebastian Steinhorst, Martin Lukasiewycz, Suhaib A. Fahmy, Samarjit Chakraborty. **Open Source Model and Simulator for Real-Time Performance Analysis of Automotive Network Security**. In: ACM SIGBED Review 13, 3 (2016), pp. 8–13. DOI: 10.1145/2983185.2983186

- Philipp Mundhenk, Sebastian Steinhorst, Martin Lukasiewycz, Suhaib A. Fahmy, Samarjit Chakraborty. **Security Analysis of Automotive Architectures using Probabilistic Model Checking**. In: Proceedings of the 52nd Design Automation Conference (DAC 2015). USA, 2015, pp. 38:1–38:6. DOI: 10.1145/2744769.2744906

- Philipp Mundhenk, Sebastian Steinhorst, Martin Lukasiewycz, Suhaib A. Fahmy, Samarjit Chakraborty. **Lightweight Authentication for Secure Automotive Networks**. In: Proceedings of the Conference on Design, Automation and Test in Europe (DATE 2015). France, 2015, pp. 1–4. DOI: 10.7873/DATE.2015.0174

- Philipp Mundhenk, Florian Sagstetter, Sebastian Steinhorst, Martin Lukasiewycz, Samarjit Chakraborty. **Policy-based Message Scheduling Using FlexRay**. In: Proceedings of the 12th International Conference on Hardware/Software Codesign and System Synthesis (CODES+ISSS 2014). India, 2014, pp. 19:1–19:10. DOI: 10.1145/2656075.2656094

- Sebastian Osswald, Daniel Zehe, Philipp Mundhenk, Pratik Sheth, Martin Schaller, Stephan Schickram, Daniel Gleyzes. **HMI Development for a Purpose-Built Electric Taxi in Singapore.** In: Proceedings of the 15th International Conference on Human-Computer Interaction with Mobile Devices and Services (MobileHCI 2013). Germany, 2013, pp. 434–439. DOI: 10.1145/2493190.2494089

The following publications are related to the topic of this thesis, but not a direct part hereof:

- Martin Lukasiewycz, Philipp Mundhenk, Sebastian Steinhorst. **Security-aware Obfuscated Priority Assignment for Automotive CAN Platforms.** In: ACM Transactions on Design Automation of Electronic Systems (TODAES) 21, 2 (2016), pp. 32:1–32:27. DOI: 10.1145/2831232.

- Martin Lukasiewycz, Sebastian Steinhorst, Sidharta Andalam, Florian Sagstetter, Peter Waszecki, Wanli Chang, Matthias Kauer, Philipp Mundhenk, Suhaib A. Fahmy, Shanker Shreejith, Samarjit Chakraborty. **System Architecture and Software Design for Electric Vehicles.** In: Proceedings of the 50th Design Automation Conference (DAC 2013). USA, 2013, pp. 95:1–95:6. DOI: 10.1145/2463209.2488852

- Licong Zhang, Debayan Roy, Philipp Mundhenk, and Samarjit Chakraborty. **Schedule Management Framework for Cloud-based Future Automotive Software Systems.** In: Proceedings of the 22nd IEEE International Conference on Embedded and Real-Time Computing Systems and Applications, (RTCSA 2016), South Korea, 2016, pp. 12–21. DOI: 10.1109/RTCSA.2016.11

- Shanker Shreejith, Philipp Mundhenk, Andreas Ettner, Suhaib A. Fahmy, Sebastian Steinhorst, Martin Lukasiewycz, Samarjit Chakraborty. **VEga: A High Performance Vehicular Ethernet Gateway on Hybrid FPGA.** In: IEEE Transactions on Computers (TC). [To Appear]

- Peter Waszecki, Philipp Mundhenk, Sebastian Steinhorst, Martin Lukasiewycz, Ramesh Karri, Samarjit Chakraborty. **Automotive Electrical/Electronic Architecture Security via Distributed In-Vehicle Traffic Monitoring.** In: IEEE Transactions on Computer-Aided Design of Integrated Circuits and Systems (TCAD). DOI: 10.1109/TCAD.2017.2666605 [To Appear]

2

Design Experience - EVA

After introducing the basic concepts of vehicle networks and security, as well as the associated challenges, this chapter will introduce the prototype electric taxi EVA. The design experience gained with EVA has significantly motivated and influenced the research presented in this work.

2.1 Introduction and Summary

EVA has been designed and built in TUM CREATE as an electric taxi for tropical megacities (see Figure 2.1). Taxis in megacities often drive large distances per day, in Singapore up to 500km in up to 24h per day. This puts severe strain on the limited battery technology available in the market today. These distances can not be achieved with conventional electric cars converted into taxis, without long breaks for charging. TUM CREATE developed EVA from ground up as an electric taxi, with a significantly larger battery than conventional electric cars and additional fast charging capabilities. Additional strain on the battery is induced by the air-conditioning, a necessity in tropical cities. EVA is equipped with an efficient overhead air-conditioning in four different climate zones, personalized for each seat.

Besides the battery and air-conditioning, EVA contains many other innovations, among them a novel infotainment system, based on smartphone interactions. While cars typically have a life time in the range of up to 10 years and development cycles of typically 7-8 years, consumer electronics changes at a far more rapid pace. Consumer electronics such as smartphones are often replaced every two years, following the rapid speed of development. This leads to vehicles with integrated infotainment systems to be outdated shortly after the start of their lifecycle.

(a) Front   *(b) Rear*

Figure 2.1: *The electric taxi EVA, built in TUM CREATE. This vehicle will serve as the design experience for a secure vehicle in this work, [171].*

To avoid this situation, EVA does not have any fixed integrated screens for passengers, but is providing services that can be used with a smartphone. The passengers can use their own smartphones and a provided app to connect to EVA and control a variety of functions. These functions include the air-conditioning, music streaming to personal speakers built into the seats and payment functions, among others.

For higher comfort of the driver and passengers and to satisfy the safety requirements, two screens have been built into EVA. These screens are constructed modular, based on tablet computers and use the same web service interface as the smartphones. This modularity, both mechanically and in software, allows to easily and cost efficiently update the screens over the lifetime of the taxi. One of the screens, the Central Information Screen (CIS) is built prominently into the center console and used as a central control point for all functions in EVA. The Instrument Cluster (IC) is placed behind the steering wheel and is used for driving and safety related information, minimizing distractions of the driver (see Figure 2.3(a)).

The use of passenger smartphones and highly integrated tablets allows the reduction of screens and computers per seat and with this a reduction in weight and electricity consumption. Furthermore, the modular concept allows fast exchanges of the built-in components, supporting cost efficient maintenance and upgrades of the system. However, allowing the passenger to connect his device to the vehicle opens an attack vector into the vehicle. In EVA, the passenger and internal networks have been connected over a gateway and firewall. While the firewall ensures that passenger devices cannot access restricted functionality, the gateway ensures the contextual correctness of the accessing device. This way, all input to the vehicle can be checked for correct content, value bounds, etc. The security in the infotainment system is build on existing standards from the Internet and computer networking domains. When trying to extend the same security protocols to the real-time networks, it became evident that little work is existing in this domain. Additionally, real-time constraints significantly complicate the introduction of security into such systems.

2.1.1 Summary

For the electric taxi EVA, a novel infotainment system has been designed and developed that allows passengers to control functions in the vehicle from their seat, while being secure. This infotainment system reduces the energy-consumption, as well as the weight of the vehicle, while ensuring full functionality, due to the reduction of screens and control elements in the vehicle.

The novel infotainment system designed for EVA inspired the approaches presented in the following chapters of this thesis. While designing and implementing the infotainment system, multiple challenges regarding the security of such a system and more general automotive architectures came to light. For these questions, the available literature did not always supply sufficient answers. These approaches will be detailed in Chapters 3 to 5.

2.2 Architecture

All interface devices (smartphones and screens) are connected via wireless networks (WiFi) to a central car server. This server consolidates and coordinates all services of the infotainment system in EVA and additionally provides the interface to the real-time networks of EVA. Besides the communication of smartphones and tablets, the server also provides access to the integrated High-Definition (HD) cameras and control of the taxi sign on the roof. The architecture is shown in Figure 2.2.

The wireless networks are split into two physically separate networks, to ensure the separation of traffic of passenger devices and internal devices, such as CIS, IC and the smartphone of the driver. Devices on the passenger network have read access to many of the functions hosted on the central server, such as location information, status of the taxi meter, etc. However, their write access is severely limited to a strictly filtered set of functions ranging from special payment service interfaces and the sound system hosted on the central server to the air-conditioning on the real-time networks via a gateway. Devices on the internal network in contrast, have significantly more rights and can, depending on the device type, write location data, start and stop the meter, override air-conditioning and sound options and lock and unlock the vehicle doors (see Table 2.1).

Every seat is equipped with stereo speakers, directly connected to the central server, resulting in eight sound channels, routed on the central server. The stereo channels can be independently controlled from the passenger smartphones (per seat), or from the CIS. Internet radio channels are available and music can be streamed from the passenger smartphone. The HD cameras are available via streams on the devices on the internal network. For possibly required proof to insurance in case of accident, the cameras additionally record in a 24h loop, whenever powered. The central server provides internet to all devices on the WiFi networks. When on the road, a cellular 4G modem is installed, in the workshop, an existing WiFi connection is used. The WiFi connection in the workshop supports further access to data loggers and the controller of the real-time networks in EVA for debugging purposes.

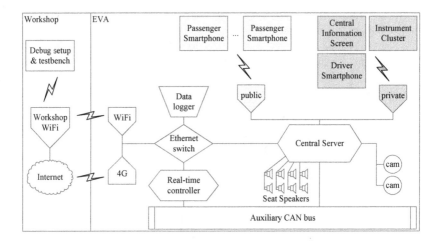

Figure 2.2: *Integration of the infotainment system inside EVA and with the automotive workshop networks. The central server hosts two WiFi networks ("public", "private") for all user interfaces to connect to. Cameras and external interfaces are connected via an Ethernet switch. Real-time controller and data logger are integrated with the infotainment system for simplified debugging. The auxiliary CAN bus of the vehicle is connected both to the central server and to the real-time controller directly.*

(a) Dashboard of EVA, including the CIS and the IC   *(b) Smartphone on the passenger armrest*

Figure 2.3: *The components of the infotainment system built into EVA, including Central Information Screen (CIS), Instrument Cluster (IC) and passenger smartphone, [171].*

Table 2.1: Examples from the Access Control List (ACL) for webservices on the central server. Public devices, such as passenger smartphones are allowed highly limited access. Private devices, such as Instrument Cluster (IC) and Central Information Screen (CIS) have significantly more access rights. Further filters are applied, based on device type or seat.

Function	Access	
	public	private
Taxi meter	read	read & write
Cameras (front/read)	read	read
Location	read	read & write
Vehicle Locks	none	read & write
Instrument Cluster theme	none	read & write
Vehicle shutdown	none	write
Emission statistics	read	read & write
Speaker volume (per seat)	read & write	read & write

2.3 Implementation

In this section, the implementation of the following four main components is described:

1. **Central Server** The central server coordinates and connects all devices in the networks.

2. **Central Information Screen (CIS)** The CIS is a touchscreen located in the center console and the main interaction point for all non-driving related controls.

3. **Instrument Cluster (IC)** The IC is the display located behind the steering wheel and displays driving-related information to the driver.

4. **Smartphones** The smartphone applications are split into driver and passenger apps. While the driver app does not contain the payment functions, the passenger app is not able to lock and unlock the vehicle.

The implementation of all devices is shortly described in the following sections.

2.3.1 Central Server

The central server forms the backbone of the infotainment system. It provides the WiFi networks, a gateway to all services in the network and interconnects all devices.

Hardware. The server is a commercial off-the-shelf (COTS) computer with Intel Core i3 processor, 2 GB of main memory and passive cooling. It is equipped with three Ethernet ports to connect the cameras on individual ports and the external connection, as well as data logger

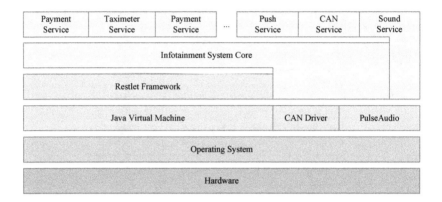

Figure 2.4: Software architecture on the central server of the EVA infotainment system. Most services rely on the message passing and task scheduling system built into the infotainment system core, which in turn is based on the Restlet framework. Some components bypass the core and the Restlet framework for direct access to components, such as the CAN bus drivers or the PulseAudio sound system.

and real-time controller on the third port. Furthermore, two MiniPCIe WiFi adapters are added as access points for the two WiFi networks. The taxi sign on the roof of the car is connected via Universal Serial Bus (USB). An additional MiniPCIe adapter acts as Controller Area Network (CAN) bus adapter. Finally, four USB sound adapters are used to connect the stereo speakers on every seat to the central server.

Software.   The infotainment system software is implemented in Java running on the Ubuntu Operating System (OS) of the server. Some parts of the software, such as the connection to the CAN bus and the support for multiple sound channels uses access to the native functions of the OS, either via C code and the Java Native Interface (JNI) or via direct execution of shell commands from Java (see Figure 2.4).

To address the sound adapters, the Linux audio system PulseAudio has been utilized. PulseAudio can be controlled via the command line and a corresponding Application Programming Interface (API) has been developed to allow control of PulseAudio from Java. The API is available as open source [110].

Components.   The software is modular and new components can be supplied in the form of Java Archive (JAR) files. These components are detected and loaded automatically at the start of the infotainment system software. An included module is responsible for updates, which can be supplied to a server and are automatically downloaded and activated after a restart of the system. Components are grouped by function and subdivided into modules and services. Modules have access to local components, such as sound adapters and the taxi sign, while services offer webservices, reachable from the devices in the vehicle. Each component is started in a separate thread of the main system. Components may start further threads, e.g. for the handling of incoming webservice requests. A watchdog service is continuously checking heartbeat signals to find non-responding threads. Due to exhaustive testing, this situation should not occur in normal operation of EVA, but cannot be avoided when prototyping new functions.

Communication. Communication between components is achieved in a Service Oriented Architecture (SOA) fashion. Components can publish and subscribe to messages via the infotainment system core. The core is also responsible for receiving messages from, filtering and passing messages to components.

Communication with devices in the infotainment system is implemented via webservices. The Restlet library is used to implement the server. The data type of webservice communication is JavaScript Object Notation (JSON). The formats of all messages have been pre-defined. Webservices are used for all non-time critical communication, starting from the devices. If time critical updates, such as location or speed are to be delivered to the device or changes in the system state are to be communicated, a User Datagram Protocol (UDP) connection is used. This connection is established on registration of the device in the vehicle.

2.3.2   Central Information Screen (CIS)

The Central Information Screen (CIS) is the main information and interaction screen prominently located in the center console of EVA.

Hardware. The CIS uses a COTS tablet as hardware platform. This reduced the development time significantly and provides a highly integrated platform. The tablet comes with additional features, which are used for different functions, such as microphone, speakers and Global Positioning System (GPS). The GPS is used, e.g., to provide location information to the central server, which in turn distributes it to all devices in the vehicle. When EVA is turned off, the CIS is turned off as well. It is started as soon as a voltage is applied to the charging port. This way, the vehicle control systems can start the CIS.

Software. The CIS uses the Android-based operating system. On top of the OS, a custom application is implemented. The application is launched automatically and runs in fullscreen. To achieve some required functions, such as power control and a custom location provider, the tablet is rooted. This allows more control over the built-in functions.

Communication. All communication in the CIS is achieved via the WiFi interface to the central server. When power to the charging port of the CIS is turned on, the tablet is configured to start automatically. On startup, the CIS registers at the central server and is assigned an identifier (ID). After registration, the CIS is usable for passengers and driver. GPS is started and location updates are pushed to the central server. There, location updates can be filtered, fused, etc. before they are sent back to the CIS via the UDP connection. On reception of the shutdown command via UDP, the CIS turns off.

2.3.3   Instrument Cluster (IC)

The IC is a screen located behind the steering wheel, providing driving-related information to the driver.

Hardware.   The IC uses the same COTS tablet as the CIS with similar settings. The internal WiFi connection is used to connect to the central server, allowing data exchange with the other devices in the infotainment system. Additionally, the IC is equipped with a Bluetooth-CAN adapter, translating commands on the control networks of EVA to messages for the tablet. This way, a direct connection between the control networks and the IC is created, reducing the amount of time before critical information is shown to the driver. While there is no direct interaction with the IC via the touchscreen, one of the levers on the steering has been dedicated to control the IC. This lever allows simple actions, such as switching the informational views in the center of the screen.

Software.   As the CIS, the IC is based on an Android-based OS. The rooted OS allows access to start and shutdown functionality, as well as custom location providers. The custom application provides the dashboard for the electric vehicle. In addition to standard values, such as speed, motor energy consumption and battery state of charge (SOC), the current status of the taxi meter is shown (free, hired, ...). Furthermore, an informational display has been integrated, allowing to switch between different views, including a map of the current location of the vehicle, as well as overall energy consumption and the rear-view camera in reverse gear. The IC also indicates any open doors in the vehicle and alerts and alarms the driver in case of faults in the car, e.g., with the high-power battery.

Communication.   Communication is implemented via WiFi and Bluetooth. As the IC is showing mostly driving related information, most data is received via Bluetooth. However, for location information and taxi meter status, the IC registers with the central server over WiFi. This process is similar to the one on the CIS above. It is important to note that beside administrative messages, the IC has no need and thus no capability to transmit messages on neither WiFi nor Bluetooth/CAN. While on WiFi this behavior can be enforced also on the side of the network, e.g., by segmenting the network and not accepting messages, there is no way to enforce this behavior on CAN. The bus relies on correct operation of all attached devices. The IC software has to be tested and trusted to behave according to the specification.

2.3.4 Smartphones

The smartphones are used by driver and passengers. They are not continuously located in EVA and can be removed. An application on the smartphone is used to connect to the vehicle and control all functions.

Hardware. For the current version of EVA we use COTS smartphones. These conventional phones are WiFi enabled and have a built-in Near Field Communication (NFC) reader. WiFi is used for communication with EVA and NFC is used to determine the seat of the passenger, based on NFC chips in the armrest of the passenger seat. The smartphone of the driver additionally includes Bluetooth, allowing to connect to the vehicle to unlock the device.

Software. Similar to the CIS and IC, the smartphones use an Android-based OS. An application is used to control all functionality in EVA. While design and overall functionality is kept similar between the driver and passenger phones, the driver phone includes additional functionality to lock and unlock EVA. In turn, it does not include payment functions. The application contains all required functions, no manual interaction by the passenger is necessary. This includes the automatic connection to the internal WiFi network of EVA and the set up of a streaming server for music streaming to the vehicle. The seat of the passenger is determined by tapping the phone on the armrest. The armrest is equipped with NFC chips, encoding the seat of the passenger as a Uniform Resource Locator (URL). Screenshots of a selection of screens are shown in Figure 2.5.

Communication. While the driver smartphone shares the internal WiFi with the built-in devices CIS and IC, the passenger smartphones use a separate network, set up by the central server. All traffic for the smartphones is routed via a Representational State Transfer (REST) API. More time-critical updates are sent via UDP. The communication constructs are similar to those of the internal devices, but are separated on the central server through the network interface of the WiFi network. This way, the smartphones are only allowed access to a non safety-critical subset of all functions in EVA (see Section 2.4.2). To determine the seat of the passenger, NFC is used.

The driver smartphone additionally uses Bluetooth for connecting to the internal real-time networks and lock/unlock or start/shutdown EVA.

2.4 Evaluation

The electric vehicle EVA has been unveiled at the Tokyo Motor Show in November 2013. After further safety tests, especially regarding the large battery, EVA has been presented to the general public in full driving functionality in April 2015. The feedback received for EVA and especially the infotainment system was enormous, ranging from local Singaporean media

(a) Location Information   (b) Radio Settings   (c) Air Conditioning

Figure 2.5: *Screenshots of the EVA smartphone app, showing (a) the location of the vehicle, (b) the settings for personal radio selection, and (c) the settings screen for the personalized air conditioning.*

outlets [126, 183] over Asian media outlets [32, 129] to well-known European and American newspapers and media outlets [82, 89, 93, 130, 169, 179]. The responses with regard to EVA's infotainment system have been positive throughout.

2.4.1   Performance

On the side of the technical performance, we separate into the devices in the vehicle:

Central Server.   Efficiency of the central server is key. As the device uses passive cooling and mounted in a confined space with limited airflow, it is required to operate as efficiently as possible. The software has been optimized as much as possible through the use of efficient software bundles and to avoid any busy wait periods. Experimental results show that the average usage of the Central Processing Unit (CPU) is in the area of 10%. Higher values are reached when utilizing the sound system. This utilization stems from PulseAudio, effectively being used as an audio mixer with multiple inputs (sources) and outputs (sinks). The software implementation lacks efficiency. The CPU utilization with playback on all seats and ten input streams can reach up to 50% of the built in Core i3 processor. With prolonged playback, the generated heat cannot be dissipated and the central server will need to shut down. Furthermore, the playback of a single input source playing on multiple seats is delayed between different seats (sinks). Thus, for prolonged multi-channel use of the system beyond the prototype stage, the software audio mixer needs to be replaced with a computer-controlled hardware option, being capable of routing sound sources without CPU overhead. As the sound system is built modular, the replacement of the components for control of a hardware mixer is trivial.

Central Information Screen (CIS). The Central Information Screen (CIS) is mostly responsible for driver information and interaction. As most computations for this are performed on the central server, the performance utilization of the device is low. However, the constantly switched-on touchscreen of the device, as well as the WiFi interconnection consume a large amount of electricity. Furthermore, the CIS is delivering the coordinates and speed of the vehicle, calculated based on the GPS signal. This requires a significant amount of power. When designing the system, the power supplied to the CIS was often not sufficient to cover these functions fully, leading to the device turning off, due to lack of power. Investigations showed high losses on the power cable included by the manufacturer. To mitigate the power losses, the charging voltage and thus the current were increased to the maximum allowed by the hardware through the vehicle power supply. The resulting charging current is able to provide sufficient energy for the CIS to operate with all functions active and additionally charge the internal backup battery. While this solution is reasonable in a prototype, the CIS is operating at the maximum of its power capabilities. For series production, it should be considered to use a dedicated GPS receiver with higher energy efficiency.

Instrument Cluster (IC). The Instrument Cluster (IC) has simple informational purposes. For this, the internal display and WiFi connection, as well as a dedicated Bluetooth connection to the vehicle CAN bus are employed. The power and CPU consumption of these components are well within the limits of the device and supplied energy.

Smartphones. Similar to the IC, the smartphones have mostly informational character, relying on the touchscreen and WiFi networks. Positioning information is transferred from the central server to the smartphone, thus GPS functionality is not required. In case of music streaming, an additional File Transfer Protocol (FTP) server service is started in the phone. However, as this is used for audio data, which typically has a low data rate, this does not significantly increase the power consumption or computation load.

2.4.2 Security

An important consideration for any infotainment system is security. As a wide range of interconnections are employed here, it needs to be ensured that these do not interfere with security concerns. E.g., it needs to be ensured that no passenger can use their smartphone to access internal functions of the vehicle, such as control over the brakes or battery. This also holds for more malicious passengers who might directly attack the vehicle with a laptop and specialized penetration software. The use of standardized connections, such as WiFi would generally allow such a behavior, thus precautions need to be taken by the developers. In the following, a selected set of precautions taken in the infotainment system of EVA shall be shortly explained:

Separate networks.   As both, internal devices (CIS, IC) and passengers, access the system over WiFi, it needs to be ensured that no unauthorized function access is possible. To achieve this, EVA uses separate WiFi networks for the internal ("private") and passenger ("public") functions. Both networks are located in individual subnets and the central server is providing two access points. The routing tables in the central server are configured such that no packets are passed between these two networks.

Separate passwords are used for the networks. The passenger network names and passwords are encoded in the NFC chips in the passengers armrest and are thus individual for every vehicle. The smartphone app developed for EVA evaluates this information and automatically connects to the correct network. The internal network passwords are stored in the internal devices (CIS, IC).

Access limitations.   All access functions and communication via devices is routed via the central server. There, an Application Level Gateway (ALG) is ensuring that devices can only access functions they are authorized for. This is done in multiple steps. Filtering based on IP address is enabled. Together with the separate networks as described above, this ensures that only devices from the right networks can access internal functions. Furthermore, a device filter is integrated, as not every device type is allowed to access every function, even inside the internal network.

Devices need to register with their type, IP address and a unique identifier at the start of the system. For internal devices, only a single device of every type (CIS, IC) is allowed access to the system. As soon as a single device of a certain type is registered, the slot for this device type is blocked and no further devices are allowed to register. This ensures that internal devices can only register at the start of the vehicle and their registration cannot be overridden by malicious passengers later, even if access to the internal WiFi is gained somehow. The unique identifier of the registered device is used in all requests to the central server, ensuring that only the permitted devices can access the functions.

Passenger smartphones follow the same setup procedure, but, contrary to internal devices, the number of smartphones that can be registered is not limited.

Data encryption.   Some broadcast push messages, such as location information, are transfered unencrypted. All other traffic is based on a Service-Oriented Architecture (SOA) and transfered over Hypertext Transfer Protocol (HTTP). This allows to easily encrypt traffic with HTTPS with conventional methods, as used on the Internet.

2.5   Concluding Remarks

The EVA infotainment system has been built as a prototype for an infotainment system for taxis, evolving around the passenger and driver. Instead of fixed mounted screens, the smartphones of the passengers are used as interfaces. This reduces the weight and power consumption of the system significantly. However, the Bring Your Own Device (BYOD) approach also triggers significant security questions, as parts of the vehicle network are opened to potentially malicious passengers. The protection of the internal networks has been realized in the form of a firewall and Application Level Gateway (ALG). However, this limits the possibilities of interactions and adds significant performance overhead on the gateway itself, which is forwarding and filtering all traffic. Furthermore, in case of a breach of this gateway or the implemented concept, the internal vehicle networks might lie open for an attacker.

In the remainder of this thesis, new approaches for security in vehicles will be highlighted, which target these gaps, by introducing security on all levels of the vehicle networks. These approaches allow to deemphasize the role of a gateway and instead focus on implementing security in a more distributed fashion. Thus, a single failure might not lead to insecurities in the overall system. Furthermore, methods to quantify security will be shown, which can be used to compare different security approaches.

Probabilistic Security Analysis for Automotive Architectures

3.1 Problem Description and Summary

Within the past two decades, the amount of electronics and software in automotive systems has increased rapidly. Today, top-of-the-range vehicles comprise up to 100 Electronic Control Units (ECUs) and several heterogeneous bus systems, implementing a variety of applications ranging from comfort to active safety functions.

While functional and safety requirements were always fundamental considerations in the design of automotive architectures, security is becoming a major challenge for many emerging applications [145]. Consumers and car manufacturers understand the benefits of cloud-connected services in vehicles, making modern infotainment systems, adaptive route planing, or over-the-air updates of software possible. However, it is also well understood that these applications present the risk of vulnerability to hacking attacks (see Chapter 1).

In current approaches, vehicle networks are shielded with firewalls at the external interfaces to ensure security. However, internal security is often not considered. Upon breach of a firewall, the network is openly accessible to the attacker. Such an example attack is illustrated in Figure 3.1.

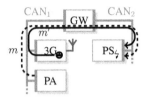

Figure 3.1: *Illustration of a possible exploit in an automotive architecture. In normal operation, the park assist (PA) controls the power steering (PS) with the message stream m that is sent via the gateway (GW). If the telematics module (3G) is hacked (●), a message stream m′ with an identical identifier $ID(m) = ID(m')$ can control the steering (↯).*

3.2   Related Work

Studies show that traditional automotive architectures that were not designed with security in mind are highly vulnerable [15, 85]. In particular, hacking a safety-critical control function can have severe and even fatal consequences. In [178], different attacks and their influence on a control function are modeled, showing that it is easily possible to tamper with driver assistance functions if their communication is not secured. Novel techniques are developed to integrate safety and security, protecting in-vehicle communication networks such as Controller Area Network (CAN) [94] and FlexRay [42]. In the automotive domain, encryption and authentication for internal buses has to be implemented efficiently, an approach to authentication has been proposed in [180].

While current state-of-the-art approaches for security in automotive systems consider separate components, the approach proposed here targets the system-level. Towards the analysis of systems, model checking has been applied to verify computer networks [140] and protocols [95]. These approaches only detect system vulnerabilities if each single component vulnerability is modeled. However, vulnerabilities are often not known at design time and, therefore, a probabilistic approach, as proposed in [10] for Denial-of-Service (DoS) exploits, can abstract this uncertainty. In [10] an approach to analyzing security protocols with probabilistic model checking based on attack cost is proposed. By contrast, we are quantizing the security of all traffic, based on the underlying automotive architecture, including DoS attacks on protocols.

Contributions.   In this chapter, we present Security Analysis for Automotive Networks (SAAN), a methodology and framework for the security analysis of automotive architectures at the system-level. We take advantage of the fact that ECU topologies, communication networks and message streams are known at design time. Using probabilistic model checking enables us to quantify the security of automotive architectures in terms of confidentiality, integrity and availability.

In Section 3.3, we outline the framework in SAAN which comprises the following three steps:

1. The considered automotive architecture is transformed into a Markov model.

2. An assessment of components is performed to determine the transition rates for the Markov model.

3. The definition of a property for the model checker is carried out to determine an appropriate security value.

With the complete Markov model and property, a probabilistic model checker determines security values for the architecture under consideration.

In Section 3.4, a detailed description of the SAAN methodology and concept is given. We increase the granularity of an architecture under test to the submodule level by including all network interfaces, bus systems, ECUs and messages. These submodules are transformed into a Markov model to transform the architecture into a graph (Section 3.4.1). The edges of the graph are weighted by probabilistic rates, representing exploitability and patching rates of each submodule. We propose to determine the rates by a standardized security assessment of every submodule separately (Section 3.4.2). Using the Markov model with assigned rates, we define properties to evaluate the architecture (Section 3.4.3). Our framework allows the definition of properties for any submodule in the architecture, thus enabling us to evaluate every security aspect relevant while considering influences of the complete architecture.

After the introduction of the concept, the implementation challenges of SAAN are discussed. In Section 3.5, our implementation of the model synthesis is described. There, we utilize the knowledge of automotive architectures, as defined in Section 3.4, to reduce the size of the resulting Markov model. We furthermore detail the subset of property specification, as required for the analysis of automotive networks (Section 3.6). After the model is synthesized and the property is defined, the model is analyzed for the property in Section 3.7. There, we reiterate the probabilistic model checking basics with a specific focus on the performance impact of different components.

The results of this analysis for a set of example architectures are presented in Section 3.8. For three architecture alternatives, we obtain and compare results. We also show the possibility to explore different exploitability and patching rates for a given architecture. Finally, we discuss the general applicability and scalability of SAAN before concluding the chapter in Section 3.9.

3.3   Framework

In the following, we give an overview of the SAAN analysis approach. After the problem description, we explain the main steps of our analysis flow.

3.3.1   Problem Description

Automotive networks consist of a high number of ECUs that perform dedicated tasks such as sensing, computation, or actuation. Functions are implemented in a distributed fashion that requires communication via different shared bus systems like CAN and FlexRay. Particularly, the communication via shared buses using predefined and often unencrypted message streams becomes a major issue once the system is compromised.

Generally, components or functions are developed independently in the automotive domain and are subsequently integrated into the architecture. While security aspects might be considered for use cases at subsystem-level, vulnerabilities at system-level are often not taken into account. As a remedy, SAAN is designed to answer the following questions during design and integration:

- What influence do component vulnerabilities have on the security of a specific function?

- Is a certain architecture design decision beneficial in comparison to an alternative in terms of security?

- How much effort should be invested in the consideration of security during implementation of specific components?

Note that we are considering system-level security, abstracting aspects of internal ECU security, such as secure boot, key storage, etc.

Since automotive architectures are highly heterogeneous systems comprising many different components, it is mandatory to model all important aspects at the system-level. For instance, communication systems used in vehicles differ greatly in their support of security aspects, particularly in terms of availability (see Section 1.3). Thus, appropriate models for these communication systems are required. ECUs might also be connected to multiple communication buses, resulting in different potential attack paths with varying probabilities. Finally, to characterize the security properties of ECUs and other components, it is necessary to quantify the rates at which they can be exploited and how fast they can, in turn, be patched. For this purpose, security assessment and Automotive Safety Integrity Level (ASIL) values should be taken into account when modeling the system.

3.3.2   Analysis Flow

Our security analysis approach for automotive architectures is outlined in Figure 3.2. It comprises three steps: Model transformation, component assessment, and property definition. Finally, the security of an architecture is determined with a probabilistic model checker.

Model Transformation.   To be able to process the architecture in terms of security, we break it down into the relevant components. These include buses, ECUs, messages, interfaces, etc.

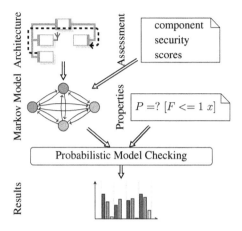

Figure 3.2: *Illustration of SAAN: (1) The architecture is transformed to a Markov model, (2) transition rates are determined by a security assessment per component and (3) a property for the model checker is defined. Finally, the probabilistic model checker returns quantified results that support decision making at the system-level.*

For each component, a Markov model defines the exploitability and patching rate. Finally, the Markov models are combined into a single system that enables probabilistic model checking. Depending on the system under consideration, this transformation can be flexibly extended or adapted. We propose a specific transformation approach in Section 3.4.1.

Component Assessment. Correspondingly to the transformation of the architecture, it is necessary to assess the individual components in terms of their exploitability and patching rates. These values determine the transition rates of the Markov model. For exploitability, we propose to use the Common Vulnerability Scoring System (CVSS) to assess the vulnerability of components, relying on an established standard [148]. Similar common criteria standards can be used with adjustments as well. Considering the ASIL values of components, we observe that patching rates strongly depend on safety requirements of components that might require costly re-testing and validation in case of software changes. These rates can be adapted by the user, depending on development processes and existing data. While the assessment should ideally be performed on subcomponent level, incorporating ECU security elements, we use a simplified component-based approach. The granularity of SAAN can be scaled up to the required level (see Section 3.9). The component assessment with CVSS and ASIL is detailed in Section 3.4.2.

Property Definition.   By defining specific properties, we are able to investigate certain aspects of the architecture in terms of security. In contrast to a steady-state analysis, which analyzes convergence to a steady state of the system at some point in time, this analysis is significantly more powerful. Thus, a property can for instance be the cumulated time that a function is exploitable within a period of 10 years. The definition of appropriate properties is detailed in Section 3.4.3.

3.4   Methodology

In this Section, we describe the methodology and concepts behind SAAN, allowing security analysis of architectures with probabilistic model checking. Specifically, the steps required to synthesize a Markov model from an architecture (Section 3.4.1), the component assessment to weight the edges of the model (Section 3.4.2), and the definition of properties to analyze the model (Section 3.4.3) are outlined.

When transforming a model from an architecture, we model ECUs and interfaces by the number of exploits existing. New exploits are discovered (e.g., by security researchers) with rate η and exploits are patched (e.g., by Over-The-Air (OTA) updates) with rate φ. These values are determined in the component assessment and will be detailed in Section 3.4.2. Networks and buses are considered passive, depending on the least secure state of all attached ECUs. Messages in turn are modeled based on the security principles of confidentiality, integrity and availability:

- *Confidentiality* describes the protection from reading messages by an unauthorized entity.

- *Integrity* describes the protection from creation and modification of messages.

- *Availability* describes protection from interruption or removal of messages.

Each of the principles is analyzed separately, depending on the protection of the message (none, cryptographic hash, encryption) and the communication networks employed for transmission.

Example.   To illustrate this process, consider a minimal architecture with a telematics ECU ($3G$ in Figure 3.2) attached to a CAN bus. The CAN bus is used to transmit a message m which is neither sent nor received by the telematics ECU. After transforming this architecture into a Markov model, we obtain the model shown in Figure 3.3. This is a very simplified synthesis, only considering telematics ECU, bus and confidentiality of m. Further, we only consider one exploit per module.

Analyzing this model, we see that from a secure state (s_0), an exploit is discovered in the telematics unit with rate η_{3G}. Once an exploit is discovered, the CAN bus is immediately considered to be exploitable (s_1). The telematics unit can be patched with rate φ_{3G}. If this does not happen and an exploit for the protection of message m, which the telematics ECU does

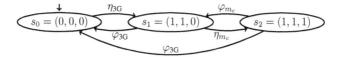

Figure 3.3: *Illustration of a simplified Markov model that analyzes the exploitability of message m in the architecture in Fig. 3.1 in terms of confidentiality with $n_{\max} = 1$. The states are composed by $s = (s_{3G}, s_{CAN_1}, s_{m_{conf}})$. Each atomic state s_i represents how many exploits for the components 3G, CAN_1, and m exist.*

not have the keys to, is discovered (with rate η_{m_c}), we advance to state s_2 and the message can be exploited. From now on, the contents of the message m cannot be considered confidential any longer, as the contents could be read and altered by an attacker. To remedy this situation, the message protection and the telematics unit should be patched. In our example model this happens with rates φ_{m_c} and φ_{3G}, respectively. Alternatively, the access for attackers can be denied by patching the telematics unit with rate φ_{3G}.

This is a very simplified example, requiring only a small subset of our proposed modeling techniques. In the following, we will explain the full set of synthesis rules, as well as the assessment of components and the analysis of the model with probabilistic properties.

3.4.1   Model Transformation

Transformation of an automotive communication architecture into a Markov model is required to be able to analyze the communication architecture with probabilistic methods. Our transformation considers all communication participants (i.e. ECUs) and interconnections (such as bus systems and networks). We further separate ECUs into interfaces for every communication system in order to analyze the impact of different communication systems. Furthermore, we analyze messages transmitted in the system.

Terminology. To model an architecture for security analysis, we require the set of all ECUs $e \in E$ and all buses $b \in B$. We also require the sets of all interfaces I_e of every ECU e. An interface $i_b \in I_e$ connects an ECU e with a bus or an external network $b \in B_e$. Thus, we define an ECU as $e = \{I_e, B_e\}$ and a bus as $b = \{E_b\}$, where E_b is the set of ECUs on bus b. To analyze a message m, the sending ECU s_m, the set of receiving ECUs R_m, and the set of buses B_m over which the message is transmitted, are required: $m = \{s_m, R_m, B_m\}$. This data is obtained from the architecture, including the fully scheduled set of messages. The maximum number of exploits considered for every module at any point in time is defined as $n_{\max}$. The relationship $x_1 \xrightarrow{\xi} x_2$ describes the change of state x_1 to x_2 with rate ξ.

ECUs & Interfaces.   To model the architecture, every ECU needs to be split into interfaces. For each interface i_b, the exploitability $\varepsilon(i_b) \geq 0$ is analyzed separately, based on the probabilistic exploitability rate η_{i_b} increasing the number of exploits n if the bus is exploitable:

$$\varepsilon(i_b) = n \xrightarrow{\eta_{i_b}} \varepsilon(i_b) = n + 1 \qquad (3.1)$$
$$\text{if } \varepsilon(b) > 0, \text{with } i_b \in I_e, 0 \leq n < n_{\max}$$

The resulting value for exploitability describes the number of parallel exploits $\varepsilon(e)$ existing in the ECU, $\varepsilon(i)$ in the interface or $\varepsilon(m)$ for the message. We use $n_{\max}$ to limit the maximum number of exploits and thus reduce the complexity of our model. The inverse of this relationship defines the patching of a security flaw in an interface i_b, based on the patching rate φ_{i_b}:

$$\varepsilon(i_b) = n + 1 \xrightarrow{\varphi_{i_b}} \varepsilon(i_b) = n \qquad (3.2)$$
$$\text{if } \varepsilon(b) > 0, \text{with } i_b \in I_e, 0 \leq n < n_{\max}$$

The exploitability of each ECU $\varepsilon(e)$ is based on the exploitability of all interfaces of this ECU:

$$\varepsilon(e) = \bigvee_{i \in I_e} \varepsilon(i) \qquad (3.3)$$

Buses & Networks.   Similarly, the exploitability $\varepsilon(b_c)$ of a CAN bus b_c is dependent on the exploitability of every attached ECU:

$$\varepsilon(b_c) = \bigvee_{e \in E_{b_c}} \varepsilon(e) \qquad (3.4)$$

In case a FlexRay bus b_f is used, additionally, the bus guardian i_{bg} needs to be exploited, before an ECU e can transmit freely on the bus:

$$\varepsilon(b_f) = \bigvee_{e \in E_{b_f}} \varepsilon(e) \wedge \varepsilon(i_{bg}) \qquad (3.5)$$

Networks or buses directly connected to the Internet, such as 3G, are always considered to be exploitable, as attackers have continuous access to these. We set a constant exploitability value of 1 to model this property:

$$\varepsilon(b_{3G}) = 1 \qquad (3.6)$$

Messages.   The exploitability of a message is subdivided into the impact categories availability A, integrity G and confidentiality C. While availability is highly dependent on the employed communication system, integrity and confidentiality are based on the message protection. Specifically, cryptographic hashing and encryption address these categories. When using a CAN bus, availability can not be guaranteed if any of the buses used for message transmission are exploited:

$$A(m) = \neg \bigvee_{b \in B_m} \varepsilon(b) \tag{3.7}$$

Confidentiality and integrity of a message m can not be guaranteed if the sending or receiving ECUs are exploited, even if the message is encrypted. To ensure real-time performance, we assume symmetric encryption, such that the key for message encryption is stored both on the sending and receiving ECUs. Secure key storage is not analyzed here, but could be integrated as a submodule into the ECU module. Confidentiality C and integrity G behave similarly, but depend on the protection mechanisms used for the respective message m. In the remainder of this section, we show the transformations for confidentiality. The rules apply identically for message integrity by replacing $C(m)/\eta_C/\varphi_C$ in the equations by $G(m)/\eta_G/\varphi_G$.

Confidentiality of a message is violated if the sender or receivers are exploitable:

$$C(m) = \neg \bigvee_{e \in \{s_m, R_m\}} \varepsilon(e) \tag{3.8}$$

Furthermore, confidentiality can be attacked by any ECU on any of the buses used for transmission of m. The probability of such an attack depends on the strength of the employed encryption algorithm and its implementation. To describe this behavior, we utilize the exploitation rate for the protection method η_C and define the following relation:

$$C(m) = 1 \xrightarrow{\eta_C} C(m) = 0 \quad \text{if } \bigvee_{b \in B_m} (\varepsilon(b)) = 1 \tag{3.9}$$

Consequently, a message is not exploitable, if all ECUs on all transmitting networks are not exploitable.

The inverse of the above operations describes the patching of a flaw in the message encryption, and is described as:

$$C(m) = 0 \xrightarrow{\varphi_C} C(m) = 1 \quad \text{if } \bigvee_{b \in B_m} (\varepsilon(b)) = 1 \tag{3.10}$$

This concludes the concept of transformation of the architecture into the states of a Markov model.

3.4.2 Component Assessment

To be able to analyze the Markov model generated in the previous section, we need to assign weights to the edges. These rates represent the probability over time that a device is exploitable and the rate in which a device can be patched.

Exploitability Rates.   In SAAN, we determine rates via an adjusted version of CVSS [148]. CVSS has been developed as an open standard to assess vulnerabilities in software systems and is maintained by the National Institute of Standards and Technology (NIST). It helps to generate a score for the security of a component, based on the assessment of units in multiple subscores and categories. The criteria used in the exploitation subscore are similar to the criteria required for interfaces in the automotive domain. We utilize the exploitation subscore (see Table 3.1) and adjust it further to adapt it to the automotive domain. Based on the scores for the subcategories, we calculate the exploitability score

$$\sigma = 20 \cdot AV \cdot AC \cdot Au. \tag{3.11}$$

Based on the exploitability score σ, we calculate the rate

$$\eta = \sigma - 1.3. \tag{3.12}$$

We normalize the exploitability rate to 1 year.

As an example, we illustrate the assessment of the 3G interface of the telematics ECU. As this device is connected to the internet, the Access Vector is across multiple networks ($AV = 1$). Due to its open surface, we assume that the device is hardened against attacks by the manufacturer, thus the access complexity is high ($AC = 0.35$). To access the device, we further assume that multiple authentication steps are required ($Au = 0.45$). From Equation (3.11), we determine $\sigma = 3.15$. Based on Equation (3.12), the exploitability rate can be determined as $\eta = 1.85$. This means that exploits for the device can be expected to be discovered 1.85 times per year.

In the remainder of the chapter, we use these CVSS-based assessments for the interfaces of all ECUs.

Patching Rates.   The amount and rate in which patches can be supplied to the vehicle is dependent on many factors. Firstly, the development time for a patch sets an upper bound to the patching rate. Additionally, the amount of tests required can be extensive, if a safety-related function needs to be altered to implement the security patch. Thus, we base our assignment of patching rates on the ASIL level of the functionality to be patched. The ASIL-dependent patching rates are shown in Table 3.2. While a safety-related device, such as the gateway (*GW*) can only be patched at relatively long intervals, non-safety-related functions, such as a telematics unit (*3G*), can be patched at short intervals, as fewer tests are required.

Using such transition rates in the Markov model allows us to analyze it on a time basis, resulting in a Continuous-Time Markov Chain (CTMC).

3.4.3   Property Definition

After creating a CTMC model from the architecture and assigning transition rates as discussed in the previous subsection, we need to define the goals of our analysis. These goals are defined

Category	Subcategory Description	Value
Access Vector (AV)	L (Local) Accessible only on device	0.395
	A (Adjacent Network) Accessible via directly attached bus	0.646
	N (Network) Accessible via any number of networks	1
Access Complexity (AC)	H (High) Device is generally secured	0.35
	M (Medium) Device is partially secured	0.61
	L (Low) Device is not secured	0.71
Authentication (Au)	M (Multiple) Multiple authentication steps required	0.45
	S (Single) One authentication step required	0.56
	N (None) No authentication is required	0.704

Table 3.1: *The categories for the CVSS exploitation subscore and interpretation of these for automotive networks (adapted from [148]).*

ASIL	patching rate (φ)	example function
A	weekly ($\varphi = 52$)	Telematics Unit
B	monthly ($\varphi = 12$)	Turning Indicator
C	bi-monthly ($\varphi = 6$)	Park Assistant
D	3-monthly ($\varphi = 4$)	Central Gateway

Table 3.2: *Assignment of patching rates to Automotive Safety Integrity Levels (ASIL). A component with higher ASIL has a higher impact on safety and thus requires more testing of software changes before an update can be rolled out.*

as properties of the model. A common property evaluated on CTMC models is a steady-state analysis. Here, the probabilities to be in each state at any sampled point in time can be calculated with conventional matrix operations. Consider the example in Figure 3.3. With rates $\varphi_{3G} = \varphi_{m_c} = 52$ (weekly) and $\eta_{3G} = \eta_{m_c} = 2$ (bi-annually), we obtain the transition rate matrix:

$$Q = \begin{pmatrix} -s_0 s_1 - s_0 s_2 & s_0 s_1 & s_0 s_2 \\ s_1 s_0 & -s_1 s_0 - s_1 s_2 & s_1 s_2 \\ s_2 s_0 & s_2 s_1 & -s_2 s_0 - s_2 s_1 \end{pmatrix} \tag{3.13}$$

$$= \begin{pmatrix} -2 & 2 & 0 \\ 52 & -54 & 2 \\ 52 & 52 & -104 \end{pmatrix} \tag{3.14}$$

Note that the values on the diagonal of the matrix are the negative sum of the rates of the row. The steady-state solution $\pi Q = 0$ yields a stationary distribution

$$\pi = \begin{pmatrix} 0.96296 & 0.036338 & 0.000699 \end{pmatrix}. \tag{3.15}$$

Consequently, at any given point in time, the probability to be in state s_2 where m is exploitable, is 0.0699%. This stationary information, however, is not conclusive for practical security questions. Thus, we are interested, e.g., in the probability that the model reaches state s_2 at least once within one year. To express this for CTMCs, we need to define a reward-based property, counting each occurence of the state. We follow the syntax in [87] and define $R\{s_2\} =? [F < 1]$ for this example. The properties required in the automotive domain will be detailed in Section 3.6.

3.5   Model Synthesis

After presenting the SAAN methodology for probabilistic model checking of automotive networks, the following sections introduce the implementation aspects and challenges. While the methodology shown above is rather straight-forward, some aspects, such as state space explosion in modeling make implementation challenging. The steps of the process, based on the methodology above, are described in the following sections.

In this section, we discuss the practical challenges that arise when synthesizing a CTMC model from an architecture. To better understand these challenges, we explore a small example. This example describes a minimal system, including a single ECU, connected via interfaces to a bus, and is depicted in Figure 3.4. Note that we split the interfaces ($i \in I$) into incoming ($g \in G$) and outgoing ($o \in O$) interfaces to demonstrate the modeling flexibility of SAAN. There, the data flow from the ECU to the bus through the outgoing interface, as well as the data flow from the bus through the incoming interface to the ECU, are shown. Furthermore, the security dependencies and the state, describing the number of exploits are depicted.

In our example in Figure 3.4, each component, except the bus, can have two different states, secure (0) or exploitable (1). Multiple exploits per device are possible but are omitted in this

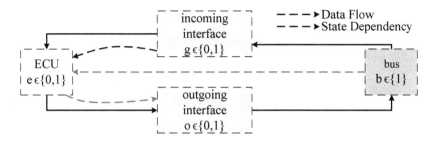

Figure 3.4: *Minimal working example for a vehicle network, including an ECU and a bus, as well as the incoming and outgoing interfaces of the ECU. Note that the data flow per path is unidirectional. Dependencies for security states are given as dashed lines.*

example for conciseness. The bus represents an always exploitable component, having only an exploitable state (1). This represents a cellular connection to the Internet, which inherently does not provide any security. In our example, the permanently exploitable bus forms the attack path into the ECU.

The number of exploits of the outgoing interface o, the ECU e and the bus b depend directly on the number of exploits of the preceding components in the data flow. In case of the incoming interface g, the state only varies with the exploitation and patching rates φ and η, as defined in Section 3.4.2. The exploitation and patching rates define how often new exploits are found and how often an exploit can be patched within a given time. The state of the incoming interface has no direct dependency on its neighbors.

When describing the architecture as above, single components and their dependencies are described. The CTMC required for model checking, however, is a combination of the states of all components and interconnections, describing the complete system at all times. When synthesizing the CTMC from these descriptions, challenges arise as the behavior of a single component is heavily dependent on the connected components.

Generic Approach. In the following, the synthesis of the CTMC, without consideration of the behavior of the automotive system as defined in Section 3.4.1, is described. The two approaches are compared in Figure 3.5. When generating the CTMC for the system with this naive approach, the model size would result in $2^3 = 8$ states (see Figure 3.6(a)), created through the combination of all possible substates, the Cartesian product. The bus has no influence on the number of states, as it has only a single possible state. Transitions between states are determined based on the exploitation (φ) and patching rates (η), as defined for the single components. We use this as a baseline for comparison with our proposed domain-knowledge approach.

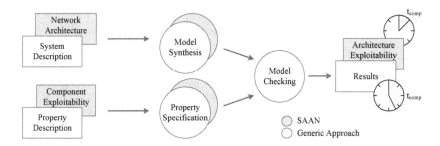

Figure 3.5: *SAAN in relation to a generic probabilistic model checker. SAAN implements a novel automated model synthesis and property specification. These use domain-knowledge about their input parameters and are thus more efficient, allowing model synthesis and checking up to three orders of magnitude faster than existing approaches (t_{comp}).*

(a) with instant transitions:

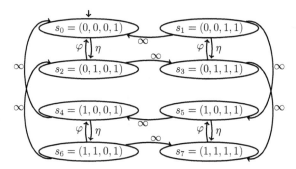

(b) without instant transitions:

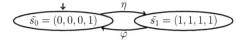

Figure 3.6: *Generic Markov model with instantaneous transitions (a) and optimized Markov model without instantaneous transitions (b) generated from the architecture in Figure 3.4. States are defined as $s_n = (s_{(n,1)}, s_{(n,2)}, s_{(n,3)}, s_{(n,4)})$, with $s_{(n,1)} = o$ being the state of the outgoing interface, $s_{(n,2)} = g$ the incoming interface, $s_{(n,3)} = e$ the ECU and $s_{(n,4)} = b$ the bus. The rates η and φ describe the exploitability and patchability of the incoming interface.*

Instantaneous Transitions. Note the transitions in Figure 3.6(a). Some component states are defined to immediately follow others (compare state dependencies in Figure 3.4) but exist as separate, intermediate states in the model. To connect these intermediate states, infinite rates (∞) are assigned to the transitions between these states. We refer to these transitions with infinite rates as *instantaneous transitions*. These transitions only exist to connect the intermediate states generated through the Cartesian product and do not directly influence the behavior of the system. To be able to compute the model, these transitions need to be approximated with large values. The chosen value for approximation has a large impact on the performance of model checking. We will discuss this impact in more detail in Section 3.7.

SAAN. While the generic approach to model generation is based on the combination of all components in the system, it is more efficient to operate on the minimal set of states describing the system. The proposed SAAN follows this efficient approach and uses the knowledge about the structure, behavior and relationships of components in a vehicle to reduce the model to its minimal size.

First, the behavior of components in relation to their neighbors is analyzed and defined in the form of rules. These rules are representing the behavior described in Section 3.4.1. Then, the states of the model are defined. Based on the Cartesian product of all component states and utilizing the set of rules, a model reduction is performed to reach the final set of states. Then, transitions between states are added, leading to the final CTMC model. These steps are explained in the following.

Rules. Rules define the behavior of components, such as shown in Figure 3.4. This behavior is formally described as rules in Equations (3.16) to (3.19) for all substates in the system. These definitions are based on the behavioral analysis in Section 3.4.1 and describe the new substate of a component depending on its former substate, as well as the states of its neighbors. By contrast to Section 3.4.1 and to reduce the model size, we do not yet consider the transitions triggered through exploitation (η) and patching (φ), but only instantaneous transitions.

The substate in a new state s' is defined as $c' \in \{e', g', o', b'\}$, depending on the component. This new substate c' relies on the previous substate of the component (in case of the incoming interface) or the previous substate of connected components (in case of all other components), as depicted in Figure 3.4. An ECU e, e.g., is always a passive component, with its state following the state of all connected incoming interfaces and the connected buses (Equation (3.16)). The incoming interface g in turn is not influenced by any connected components (Equation (3.17)). While the state of the outgoing interface o is based on the state of the ECU (Equation (3.18)), the state of the bus b is based on the state of all outgoing interfaces (Equation (3.19)).

$$e_x' = \sum_b (g_x^{(b,e)} \cdot b), \qquad e_x, e_x' \in E \tag{3.16}$$

$$g_x^{(b,e)'} = g_x^{(b,e)}, \qquad g_x^{(b,e)}, g_x^{(b,e)'} \in G \tag{3.17}$$

$$o_x^{(e,b)'} = e, \qquad o_x^{(e,b)}, o_x^{(e,b)'} \in O \tag{3.18}$$

$$b_x' = \bigvee_e o_x^{(e,b)}, \qquad b_x, b_x' \in B \tag{3.19}$$

While Equation (3.19) describes the general behavior of a bus, as we will use it in the evaluation in Section 3.8, note that in our minimal example, the bus is always exploitable, as it forms the attack path: $b_x' = b_x = 1$ (compare Equation (3.6)).

As can be seen from the above rules, the incoming interface is the only component not instantaneously depending on others. It follows that exploits and patches are applied to this component with rates η and φ. This models the behavior that an attacker can only attack an ECU through incoming connections. In case of multiple incoming interfaces, multiple attack paths with a differing number of exploits are possible.

Initial States.   Every component contains an initial state. For most components, this should be the secure state (0). Some components, however, such as a cellular connection, can be considered to start in an exploitable state (1) or even contain constantly exploitable states, such as the bus in Figure 3.4. The set of initial states of all components forms the initial state of the system.

State Reduction.   To raise the efficiency of the model checking approach, we apply the rules defined above to reduce the model to the minimum number of states. The minimal set of states describing the behavior of the system without instantaneous transitions can be determined by reducing the set of all states with instantaneous transitions. Equation (3.20) describes the set of all possible states by creating the Cartesian product of all component states.

$$S = E \times G \times O \times B \tag{3.20}$$

Based on a single state $s \in S$, a function is required that maps the set of all states to a subset which contains all states without instantaneous transitions:

$$f : S \to S \tag{3.21}$$

$$S' = f(S) = \{f(s)|s \in S\}, S' \subseteq S \tag{3.22}$$

For our example, this function can be easily defined over the components in the system:

$$f(s) = f(o_x^{(e,b)}, g_x^{(b,e)}, e_x, b_x) = (o_x^{(e,b)'}, g_x^{(b,e)'}, e_x', b_x') \tag{3.23}$$

The resulting changes for component states can be calculated from the set of rules for all components (see Equations (3.16) to (3.19)). Here, the new state is calculated based on the current states. Note that it needs to be ensured that only unique combinations of component states and thus unique states s' are contained in S'.

Transitions. Once the model reduction is complete and the minimal set of all states has been found, these states need to be connected via transitions. Adding these transitions is trivial. A transition from a state s_1 to a state s_2 is added whenever no more or less than a single transition exists, which can trigger the state change through exploitation or patching. For example, between states $(0, 0, 0, 1)$ and $(1, 1, 1, 1)$, only a single component can independently change its state for the transition to occur, namely the incoming interface g. All other component states follow the change of i based on the defined rules (see Figure 3.6(b)). The rates for the transitions are defined as the exploitation rates η and patching rates φ of components.

Example. Applying the above mapping function to our example in Figure 3.4, starting from $s_0 = (0, 0, 0, 1)$, a transition of the incoming interface $g' = 1$ with η leading to intermediate state $(0, 1, 0, 1)$ triggers the substate change of the ECU (see Equation (3.16)) $e'_x = 1$, resulting in intermediate state $(0, 1, 1, 1)$. The transition of the ECU in turn triggers the substate transition of the outgoing interface (see Equation (3.18)) to $o' = 1$, resulting in a state change to $s' = s_1 = (1, 1, 1, 1)$. As all rules are applied in a single step, the intermediate states are no longer required in the model (see Figure 3.6(b)).

This concludes the synthesis of model from architecture. In the next section, we specify properties used to evaluate the model generated here.

3.6 Property Specification

To evaluate the model synthesized in Section 3.5, a property needs to be specified. The model is then checked for the property by a model checking algorithm. In case of generic approaches, a large number of diverse properties can be defined. Typically, a language, such as Computation Tree Logic (CTL), is employed to formalize the description of properties. Properties that can be verified are very flexible and include, among others, reachability and the time the system remains in a certain set of states.

For SAAN, we are primarily interested in the time a system, subsystem, component or a combination of these are exploitable. To determine this, we need to define the analysis time t and the states of interest $\bar{\rho}$ as property ϕ:

$$\phi = \{\bar{\rho}, t\}. \tag{3.24}$$

While the definition of time t is straight-forward, the states of interest are defined as the vector $\bar{\rho}$. For this, we call the components to be analyzed $c \in C$. As exploitability corresponds to the time that a given system remains in a single state or a set of states, we summarize these states in a vector $\bar{\rho}$. Vector $\bar{\rho}$ has the same length as the number of states in the system: $|\bar{\rho}| = |S|$. For every substate $s_{(n,c)}$ of components to analyze (see Figure 3.6), the corresponding value in the vector is set to one, if the substate is exploitable, or else to zero:

$$\bar{\rho} = \rho(s_n), \forall s_n \in S \tag{3.25}$$

$$\rho(s_n) = \begin{cases} 1, & \text{if } \exists c \in C : s_{(n,c)} > 0 \\ 0, & \text{else} \end{cases} \tag{3.26}$$

When analyzing the state of the ECU in our example in Figure 3.6(b) for exploitability ($s_{(1,3)}$), this leads to $C = \{3\}$ and $\bar{\rho} = \left(\begin{smallmatrix} 0 \\ 1 \end{smallmatrix}\right)$.

In the next section we present the model checking algorithm, verifying the properties of the model and using the synthesized model and the property specification as input.

3.7   Model Checking

After determining the model to be analyzed in Section 3.5 and specifying a property in Section 3.6, in this section, we analyze the model for the specified property ϕ. The analysis we apply is based on [86] and will be briefly introduced here.

Here, the focus is on probabilistic model checking for CTMCs. In the following, the elements required for model checking of CTMCs are reproduced in their adjusted and simplified forms from [86] (Equations (3.27) through (3.34)). In the process, some elements will be highlighted, as these are crucial for a well-performing model checking.

The input to the model checking algorithm is a matrix Q, describing the model, and the property ϕ to be checked for. The property ϕ contains the vector $\bar{\rho}$, describing the set of states to be analyzed and the analysis time frame t. The matrix Q describes the transitions by assigning the rate $R(x, y)$ of the transition at the coordinates (x, y) in the matrix for a transition from state x to state y. A transition from y to x is noted at (y, x) accordingly. Non-existing transitions between states have a rate of zero and are set accordingly in Q. Another requirement for the matrix is that rows sum up to zero. Thus, the value at (x, x) is set to the negative sum of all items in the row:

$$Q(x, y) = \begin{cases} R(x, y) & x \neq y \\ -\sum_{w \neq x} R(x, w) & x = y \end{cases} \tag{3.27}$$

In the following, we will shortly explore the matrix generation for the generic approach in Figure 3.6(a) as Q_{gen} and for SAAN as Q_{SAAN}. For the exploitation and patching rates, we define $\eta = \varphi = 2$. As described in Section 3.5, infinite transition rates, such as required in Figure 3.6(a), need to be approximated for the generic approach. In the following, we use a value of 10. The resulting matrices for our minimal example from Figure 3.6(a) and (b) are shown in Equations (3.28) and (3.29), respectively.

$$
Q_{gen} = \begin{pmatrix}
-2 & 0 & 2 & 0 & 0 & 0 & 0 & 0 \\
10 & -12 & 0 & 2 & 0 & 10 & 0 & 0 \\
1 & 0 & -11 & 10 & 0 & 0 & 0 & 0 \\
0 & 1 & 0 & -11 & 0 & 0 & 0 & 10 \\
10 & 0 & 0 & 0 & -12 & 0 & 2 & 0 \\
0 & 0 & 0 & 0 & 10 & -12 & 0 & 2 \\
0 & 0 & 10 & 0 & 1 & 0 & -21 & 10 \\
0 & 0 & 0 & 0 & 0 & 1 & 0 & -1
\end{pmatrix}
\tag{3.28}
$$

$$
Q_{SAAN} = \begin{pmatrix} -2 & 2 \\ 1 & -1 \end{pmatrix}
\tag{3.29}
$$

The matrix, as representation of the CTMC, is checked over the given time t. To do so, the process from [86] is applied. First, the matrix Q needs to be normalized. To achieve this, the matrix Q is divided by q, the maximum of all outgoing transitions of a state. This value can be found as the absolute maximum of all values in Q:

$$
\arg \max_x \{ q = |Q(x, x)| \}.
\tag{3.30}
$$

As the application here always contains positive rates, $q \leq 0$ does not need to be considered.

Following Definition 12 in [86], the resulting matrix $P^{\mathrm{unif}} = I + \frac{Q}{q}$, where I is the identity matrix, represents the uniformized Discrete Time Markov Chain (DTMC) embedded in our analyzed CTMC. As P^{unif} considers all transition rates in a single time step, $(P^{\mathrm{unif}})^m$ considers all transition rates between states within m time steps.

To model the transitions, exponential distributions are assumed in CTMCs To model this exponential behavior, a Poisson distribution (γ) is employed in every step. The parameters for the distribution are set to $\lambda = q \cdot t$ and $k = m$, thus modeling the distribution of rates with q, triggering m times within t. The cumulative Poisson probabilities are required to model the exponential behavior.

This allows us to calculate the transition matrix over time t:

$$
\Pi_t = \sum_{m=0}^{\infty} \gamma_{m, q \cdot t} \cdot (P^{\mathrm{unif}})^m
\tag{3.31}
$$

This however, does not yet allow the direct knowledge of the probability of a single state after time t. Thus, vector ρ is created to select the states of interest by setting the corresponding value of the vector to 1. Following Proposition 4 in [86] yields

$$
\Pi_t = \sum_{m=0}^{\infty} \overline{\gamma}_{m, q \cdot t} \cdot (P^{\mathrm{unif}})^m \cdot \rho
\tag{3.32}
$$

with

$$\overline{\gamma}_{m,q \cdot t} = \frac{1}{q} \cdot (1 - \sum_{j=m}^{m} \gamma_{j,q \cdot t}) \tag{3.33}$$

The expected value is finally defined to be:

$$E_t = \sum_{m=0}^{\infty} \frac{1}{q} \cdot (1 - \gamma_{m,q \cdot t}) \cdot (P^{\text{unif}})^m \cdot \rho \tag{3.34}$$

In the following, we will briefly discuss the performance implications of this computation.

Performance Implications.   While the computation in Equation (3.34) is defined as an infinite sum, in reality, this computation will have to be bounded. Typically, the algorithm in [35] is used to determine the minimum and maximum number of iterations required to achieve a set accuracy. There, the number of iterations is defined as linearly proportional to $q \cdot t$ for large $q \cdot t$. If existing, instantaneous transitions, by definition, form the largest rates in the system. This leads to a larger number of iterations in Equation (3.34) and thus longer computation times. This dependency clearly shows the influence of large approximations for instantaneous transitions on the computation time of the model checking algorithm. Thus, q should be kept as small as possible.

Furthermore, too large approximations for instantaneous transitions can lead to a stiff model, when the smallest and largest rate in the system differ too much, in our setup around 7 orders of magnitude or more. Too small approximations, however, result in inaccurate results, as they do not represent reality accurately. In any case, instantaneous transitions will lead to a larger q, slowing down model checking. Our proposed SAAN eliminates instantaneous transitions and consequently improves model checking efficiency.

Model Size.   The generic approach results in significantly larger models than the domain-specific approach, as shown in Equations (3.28) and (3.29), respectively. Analyzing larger models increases analysis time, as the matrix multiplication in Equation (3.34) takes significantly longer. Removing instantaneous transitions reduces the model size, thus minimizing the computations required for model analysis. This will be analyzed in Section 3.8.3.

3.8   Experimental Results

In this section, we discuss our experimental setup and show the potential of our analysis methodology by applying the framework to a case study based on the three architectures illustrated in Figure 3.7. The analysis of the architectures, modeled with the methodology introduced in Section 3.4, is performed with the probabilistic model checking tool PRISM [87].

The computations for one property in the architectures and with $n_{\max} = 2$ require between 15 minutes and 1.5 hours on a conventional desktop computer with an Intel Xeon quad-core

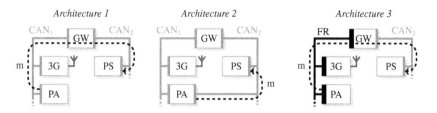

GW - gateway, PS - power steering, PA - park assist, 3G - telematics unit, CAN - controller area network, m - message stream, FR - FlexRay

Figure 3.7: *Three architectures used to compare different approaches to security. Architecture 1 transmits message m on the same bus as the telematics unit is located. Architecture 2 adds a dedicated connection for message m. Architecture 3 introduces a FlexRay bus for the transmission of message m.*

processor at 3.2 GHz. Every PRISM computation runs as a single process with negligible memory usage. The runtime correlates with the number of states in the generated Markov model. The models for our example architectures in Figure 3.7 have between 400,000 and 1.2 million states. All results are given as the percentage of time the message m is exploitable within 1 year.

3.8.1   Architecture Evaluation

We evaluate three different architectures that are based on real-world systems. We only consider a relevant subsystem of the complete vehicle architecture as illustrated in Figure 3.7. The considered architectures comprise two bus systems connected by a gateway, a telematics unit, and an automatic parking assistance application, including 2 ECUs. The automatic parking assistant has been reduced to one message stream transmitted between the parking assistant controller and the power steering of the vehicle.

Architectures and Component Assessment. Architecture 1 resembles the example in Figure 3.1. Since it is assumed that the security of this system is not optimal, we also consider two alternative architectures. In Architecture 2, the message stream m is sent via an additional connection directly on CAN_2, avoiding an exposure of the stream on the bus that is directly connected to the telematics unit. In Architecture 3, we replace the CAN bus with a time-triggered FlexRay bus where a schedule is defined at design time with a fixed assignment of slots to devices.

The exploitation and patching rates for our examples can be found in Table 3.3. We assume that critical ECUs, such as the gateway and the telematics unit, are hardened against attacks. The exploitation rate of message m depends on the security features used. We consider three variants: Unencrypted, Cipher-based Message Authentication Code (CMAC) with 128 bit key and Advanced Encryption Standard (AES) with 128 bit key. While an unencrypted message is

Module	Interface	η (CVSS v2 Vector)	φ (ASIL)
Park Assistant (PA)	$CAN_1/CAN_2/FR$	1.2 *(AV:A/AC:H/Au:S)*	12 *(C)*
Power Steering (PS)	CAN_2	1.2 *(AV:A/AC:H/Au:S)*	4 *(D)*
Gateway (GW)	$CAN_1/CAN_2/FR$	1.2 *(AV:A/AC:H/Au:S)*	4 *(D)*
Telematics (3G)	CAN_1/FR	3.8 *(AV:A/AC:L/Au:S)*	52 *(A)*
	3G	1.9 *(AV:N/AC:H/Au:M)*	52 *(A)*
FlexRay Bus Guardian (BG)	local	0.2 *(AV:L/AC:H/Au:S)*	4 *(D)*
Message (m)	unencrypted	∞ (instant)	-
integrity	CMAC128	1.2 *(AV:A/AC:H/Au:S)*	-
	AES128	1.2 *(AV:A/AC:H/Au:S)*	-
Message (m)	unencrypted	∞ (instant)	-
confidentiality	CMAC128	∞ (instant)	-
	AES128	1.2 *(AV:A/AC:H/Au:S)*	-

Table 3.3: Results of the security assessment for exploitation rates and patching rates. Devices such as gateway, telematics unit and FlexRay Bus Guardian are specifically hardened against attacks. Message assessment depends on the mode to be evaluated (integrity, confidentiality). Message availability is addressed through the underlying bus system.

instantly exploitable, a CMAC protected message provides integrity, while an AES protected message can ensure confidentiality.

The patching rates for all devices are based on the ASIL evaluation. The resulting values are listed in Table 3.3.

Results. The results of our analysis are illustrated in Figure 3.8. It can be observed that cryptographic hashing with CMAC 128 only improves security in terms of integrity while encryption with AES 128 is effective for integrity and confidentiality. This validates our results as cryptographic hashing only prevents creation of messages while encryption also prevents reading.

In general it can be observed that neither cryptographic hashing nor encryption improves the security values significantly. This is a counter-intuitive result that can be explained as follows: By hacking the Park Assist (PA), the cryptographic hashing and encryption, respectively, are compromised and lose their effectiveness. Particularly the relatively low patching rate of the PA due to its ASIL values results in a high exploitability of the device.

It can further be observed that Architecture 2 does not improve the security significantly in comparison with Architecture 1 and in some cases it even becomes worse. Here, the low patching rates of the PA and the Gateway (GW) lead to high exploitabilities of these devices,

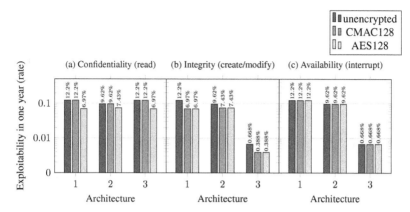

Figure 3.8: *Results of the analysis of the architectures shown in Figure 3.7. We analyze message m in terms of Confidentiality, Integrity and Availability for different protection mechanisms (unencrypted, CMAC 128, AES 128) across all three architectures. Results clearly show less exploitation potential for better encryption and more carefully designed architectures. In terms of availability, support from the bus system is required to ensure reasonable security.*

resulting in an exposed CAN$_2$. At the same time, the PA in Architecture 2 is exposed to two buses resulting in higher exploitability. Connecting the PA to CAN$_2$ might even result in further security issues as the device might be exploited as a bridge to attack other functions. This would result in a significantly worse security value for Architecture 2 for functions that are implemented on CAN$_2$ only.

In FlexRay, the existing bandwidth is divided in a time-triggered manner. Devices can only transmit in their slot and are denied by the bus guardian to transmit in other slots. This safety measure also has a significant security impact as devices can not maliciously transmit messages in other timeslots. This leads to an overall reduction of the attack surface as devices which are part of the communication or the bus guardian need to be infiltrated to attack message m.

3.8.2   Parameter Exploration

To evaluate the effect of different exploitability rates and patching rates, we analyze the sensitivity of the exploitability of message m in Architecture 1 to these rates for the entrance point ECU *3G*. As the *3G* ECU is the entrance point to the architecture, the exploitation rate of message m heavily depends on the exploitation and patching rates for the *3G* ECU. We independently analyze exploitation and patching rates between once per decade ($\eta_{3G} = \varphi_{3G} = 0.1$) and once per hour ($\eta_{3G} = \varphi_{3G} = 8760$). When varying the exploitation rate, the patching rate is set to $\varphi_{3G} = 52$; when varying the patching rate, the exploitation rate is set to $\eta_{3G} = 1.9$. The re-

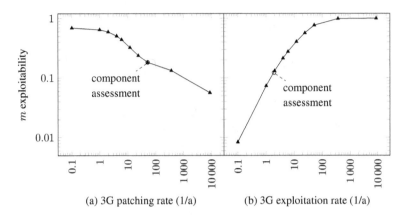

(a) 3G patching rate (1/a)   (b) 3G exploitation rate (1/a)

Figure 3.9: *Exploration of parameters to evaluate influence on complete architecture security. In (a), the patching rate of the entrance point is varied, while in (b), different strengths of security are employed in the telematics ECU forming the start point to a vehicle attack.*

sults are shown in Figure 3.9. They exhibit exponential behavior. Hence, we can conclude that while changes at the lower end of the exploitation resistance/patching spectrum have a rather large impact on the system, higher rates do not significantly help optimize security. Assuming a threshold of 0.5% exploitability, a reasonable patching rate for an internet-connected ECU without other access methods would be around $\varphi = 6$ (every 2 months). In case the exploitation rate is reduced by further securing the device, an exploitation rate of maximum $\eta = 12$ (once a month) needs to be guaranteed to keep exploitability under 0.5%. Patching rates of $\eta = 12$ are common also in other domains, such as consumer electronics and software.

Such an analysis can be performed for every element in the architecture. Thus, depending on the architecture, devices can either be hardened against attacks or patching rates can be contractually agreed upon between the Original Equipment Manufacturer (OEM) and suppliers.

3.8.3 Scalability

To evaluate our approach for scalability, we generate multiple architectures of different sizes and verify these with SAAN and its model reduction as defined in Section 3.5. For comparison, we input the same architectures into a generic probabilistic model checking tool, in our case PRISM. All calculations have been performed on a workstation with Intel Xeon E5-1620 at 3.60GHz and 32GB RAM.

The evaluation starts from a single bus with two connected ECUs. The ECUs have been modeled with interfaces as shown in Figure 3.4. For our measurements, we increase the number of ECUs in this basic system. All ECUs are connected to the same bus. The evaluation is stopped as soon as the framework under test (SAAN, PRISM) reaches the timeout of one hour. The property to be checked is defined as the time the outgoing interface of the first ECU is exploitable.

The results are shown in Figure 3.10 on a logarithmic scale. It is clearly visible that SAAN outperforms PRISM in terms of computation time in all test cases by two to three orders of magnitude. Furthermore, the matrix size is up to five orders of magnitude smaller in SAAN than in PRISM. Some of the computation time advantages gained through the smaller matrix size in SAAN are absorbed by the more complex computations required for model synthesis, thus leading to a speed-up of two to three orders of magnitude for the five orders of magnitude in matrix size.

While PRISM reaches the set timeout of one hour after only 6 additional ECUs, SAAN manages to encompass 10 additional ECUs in the system. Thus, SAAN is able to operate on complete functional clusters. Note that the matrix size in SAAN reaches the same orders of magnitude PRISM requires for one additional ECU only when adding nine ECUs.

Note that the property to be evaluated and the automotive architecture chosen have an impact on the computation time. The influence of the selected property ϕ to evaluate is two-fold. On the one hand, the selection vector $\bar{p}$ is a simple vector multiplication and has minimal influence on the computation time. On the other hand, ϕ contains the time t to analyze. This has significant influence on the number of iterations and thus the computation time. An increasing analysis time increases the number of iterations and thus the computation time. This holds for both approaches and increases the performance gap further, as the time for one iteration is highly dependent on the matrix multiplication $(P^{\text{unif}})^i$ and thus, the number of states. However, the number of iterations is also proportional to the largest transition in the system (see Section 3.7). Thus, even for small t, the instantaneous transitions in the generic approach will lead to longer computations times than in SAAN.

The chosen architecture further impacts the computation time, as larger architectures offer a larger potential for state space reduction. Typically, states can be reduced for every component in the system, thus the model size is growing more rapidly in the generic approach than in SAAN. However, even for small architectures, such as with three ECUs and one bus, the computation time advantage is two orders of magnitude, as shown in Figure 3.10.

In summary, the domain-specific approach targeted to the automotive domain allows a performance increase of multiple orders of magnitude over generic solutions for identical architecture input. This enables the designed to verify the security of complete functional clusters with up to 12 ECUs.

3.9 Concluding Remarks and Future Work

In this work we have proposed a methodology for security analysis of automotive communication architectures. By analyzing the system-level architecture at design-time, we can quantify

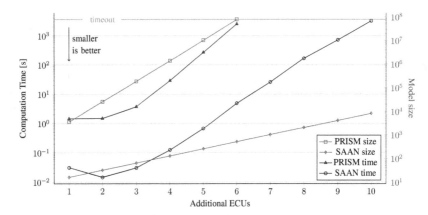

Figure 3.10: *Comparison of synthesized model size and computation time of a generic model checker (PRISM) with SAAN. Computation time includes model synthesis and checking. Lower values are better. SAAN clearly outperforms PRISM in both computation time and matrix size.*

the security of every element in terms of confidentiality, integrity and availability. The results of this analysis can help in design decisions for the overall architecture and the security capabilities of components. For the first time, the impact of individual components on the overall security of an architecture can be determined. We analyze an architecture by generating a corresponding Markov model. Edge weights are determined through a security assessment of components. We define security properties and analyze these over the model with a probabilistic model checker. The results show that this method can be used to find security flaws in architectures, which cannot be identified at the component or subsystem level. Implementation challenges, such as scalability and performance issues have been addressed by the implementation of a model reduction in the synthesis and a targeted model checker for application of automotive networks. We introduce a set of rules, describing the security dependencies in existing networks. With this, we are able to decrease model sizes by up to five orders of magnitude and computational time for model synthesis and checking by up to three orders of magnitude.

Future work will seek to improve performance further. With this, we will be capable of analyzing more fine grained models and more complex systems, e.g., comprising Ethernet. Furthermore, we will be able to generate a set of best practices for automotive architectures, based on our security analysis. A combination of security and reliability analysis, as well as the integration of ECU internal security measures is planned. Additionally, we will employ the SAAN framework as evaluation basis to optimize vehicle networks based on security.

4

Lightweight Authentication Framework

4.1 Problem Description and Summary

The rapidly increasing connectedness of modern cars leads to new challenges in the security of inter- and intra-vehicle communication. As increasing numbers of vehicles are being connected to the outside world, the exposure risk of safety-critical systems rises significantly. With the multitude of communication interfaces, it is very difficult, or even impossible, to reliably control all entry points into the vehicle or shield the vehicular network with firewalls. Hence, it is important that, besides the external access points, communication within a vehicle is secured. This does not only hold if the external protections are breached, but also for targeted attacks, e.g., via the internal On-Board Diagnosis (OBD) port, the infotainment system or the telematics unit. With the introduction of networked comfort and entertainment functions, as well as Advanced Driver Assistance Systems (ADASs), vehicles are more readily connected to external networks, such as car-to-x networks and the Internet. This trend towards interconnectivity continues in the vehicle interior. Increasingly, passengers and drivers connect smartphones and other mobile devices to the vehicle and perform comfort and control functions, such as music streaming, phone access, but also vehicle related functions, such as control of air-conditioning and the vehicle locks. This increase in interconnections also raises the attack surface of the vehicle. This holds especially for the integration of vehicles in car-to-x networks. In these networks, safety-critical data is transmitted, allowing deep insights into the state of a car and high influence on other cars. The impact of a malicious attack on automotive safety-critical systems can be devastating, including high financial damages and even loss of life. To mitigate the effects of such attacks, protection mechanisms have been developed to limit unauthorized access to in-vehicle communication and minimize the number of attack vectors [114, 39, 173, 177]. To allow real-time behavior, these protection mechanisms are based on symmetric cryptography, requiring pre-shared keys. Pre-programming these keys opens another attack vector, especially if the same keys are used throughout the lifetime of a vehicle and across multiple vehicles. Thus, it is necessary to generate and exchange keys at runtime. Only by using dynamic keys and limiting the duration of key validity, can secure in-vehicle communication be provided.

Security. It is to be noted that no security mechanism can be considered 100% secure. Security is highly dependent on the capabilities (computational, knowledge) of an attacker, which typically develop over time. However, the security of a concept, such as a protocol, at the time of development can be formally verified. This ensures that the protocol is free of flaws that allow circumvention. Formal verification of the proposed protocols is presented in this work.

The level of security of any measure further depends on the algorithms and parameters chosen for protection. The algorithms are typically either of symmetric (with pre-shared key) or asymmetric (without pre-shared key) type. The parameters depend on the algorithms and include for almost all algorithms the length of the encryption key, as well as for some algorithms the chosen encryption basis, e.g., the exponent in case of RSA or the parameters for the selected curve in Elliptic Curve Cryptography (ECC).

Typically, security is analyzed across the metrics of confidentiality, integrity, and availability. In terms of network communication, confidentiality describes the security of a message against being read by an attacker. Integrity describes protection against creation or alteration of messages, and availability describes the security against interruption of messages. In this work, we seek to enable the protection of all three aspects through a secure key exchange, allowing the distribution of keys to Electronic Control Units (ECUs), which in turn are enabled to encrypt their messages, thus adhering to confidentiality and integrity. At the same time, the authentication of ECUs and authorization of message streams helps to ensure that only legitimate ECUs can participate in the communication and perpetrators are easier to detect, thus enabling simplified enforcement of availability.

LASAN. The structure of the proposed Lightweight Authentication for Secure Automotive Networks (LASAN) is shown in Figure 4.1. It consists of the core protocol concepts presented in Section 4.3. It is optimized for the message distribution and architectures in the automotive context, specifically fixed networks and multicast messages. LASAN further includes the protocols and procedures to be integrated with the automotive life cycle, making it a usable protocol. These considerations are detailed in Section 4.4. This enables necessary features required for the application of the protocol to real-world scenarios, such as the exchange of ECUs. LASAN is verifiable for security and can be evaluated regarding its real-time capabilities.

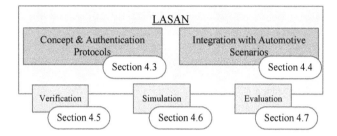

Figure 4.1: *The Lightweight Authentication for Secure Automotive Networks (LASAN) consists of the protocols, as well as the protocols and processes required to integrate these authentication protocols into automotive scenarios. We verify and evaluate LASAN for security and performance to show its superior qualities over existing protocols.*

4.1.1 Challenges and Opportunities

In automotive networks, the primary focus is on real-time capabilities to support control systems, which need to respond within a given short time, so predictability and reliability are the dominating factors. At the same time, ECUs have significantly less computational resources than modern computer systems and automotive networks have significantly lower data rates than their consumer counterparts. Maintaining predictability with low-powered ECUs and low data rates while adding security is challenging since many existing security approaches assume greater computational capacity or higher bandwidth than is available. To overcome this challenge, we divide the required security actions into two groups: those that are time-critical for the vehicle's operation, and those that can be performed asynchronously without affecting security properties. This allows the system to achieve the required real-time performance and maintain the desired level of security (see Section 4.3).

A further challenge for security in automotive use cases is that connectivity may be intermittent. While cars are increasingly interconnected, this access is not available to all ECUs in the network. This is of course a security measure in itself, to shield ECUs from potential attacks. To overcome this challenge, we use asymmetric cryptography and certificates to allow components to make security decisions without requiring connectivity to external parties (see Section 4.4).

Lastly, messages in automotive networks are typically multicast or broadcast messages, reaching many or all receivers at the same time. This behavior is not typical for consumer networks and thus, there is only limited support in existing security protocols. We enhance existing protocols with the ability to authorize messages for multiple receivers, through the introduction of a root of trust in the network, the security module (see Section 4.3).

Further, it is important to note that automotive networks are defined at design time and typically do not change over the lifetime of a vehicle. We utilize this fact by reducing flexibility in the security framework, based on the reasonable assumption that all devices run the same version of our proposed security framework. Reducing flexibility and focusing on a static network allows us to reduce message sizes significantly. As encryption/decryption and transmission of the initial messages take large amounts of time, this reduction leads to a system with much lower latencies (see Section 4.7).

In the following, we describe in detail how we address these challenges and exploit the opportunities for a secure and lightweight authentication framework.

4.1.2   Contributions

In this work we analyze the design aspects required for security in automotive networks at the system level. As the security of any system is highly dependent on the implementation and interaction with other components, it is indispensable to integrate the security components well with the overall system. We demonstrate how the authentication protocols can facilitate this integration. We further verify and evaluate the framework to prove its security and real-time capabilities, required in the automotive domain.

1. We developed the protocols of the LASAN required to securely authenticate and authorize devices and messages (Section 4.3). We further show the full integration into the automotive life cycle (Section 4.4), thus, e.g., enabling secure exchange of ECUs. To the best of our knowledge, LASAN is the only published protocol shown to be fully compatible with current automotive processes.

2. We analyze the security properties of the proposed protocols using established protocol verification techniques. Specifically, we model and analyze the protocols using the Scyther tool [18] (Section 4.5).

3. We have built a discrete event simulator for automotive networks (see Section 4.6) and we use it to analyze the latencies and bandwidth requirements of LASAN with respect to the real-time constraints of this domain (Section 4.7). This simulator is further used to quantify the performance of LASAN in comparison to two existing authentication frameworks, Transport Layer Security (TLS) and Timed Efficient Stream Loss-Tolerant Authentication (TESLA).

4.2   Related Work

To reduce the risk from pre-shared keys, authentication frameworks have been developed in other domains, such as corporate networks and the Internet, allowing the exchange of keys without prior interaction of the communication participants.

Kerberos and TLS.   Examples include Kerberos [119] and the widely used Secure Sockets Layer (SSL)/TLS framework [23]. Kerberos can be extended to a two-phase system to initialize the system with public-key mechanisms [184]. These mechanisms have been designed for use in computer networks and have significant overheads, preventing their efficient use in real-time systems. They allow the exchange of keys without prior knowledge of the communication participants by adding an element of trust in the network. This can be a trusted server on the Internet or a specially secured ECU in vehicle networks. However, as we will show, the real-time performance of such mechanisms, as well as their fundamentally different orientation towards Internet communications makes these frameworks unsuitable for the automotive domain (see Section 4.7).

TESLA.   The TESLA system has been designed specifically for low-performance communication systems [133]. In TESLA, the sender generates a new symmetric key and computes the Message Authentication Codes (MACs) for one or more messages. After the messages have been received, the sender broadcasts the key on the bus, allowing every recipient to authenticate the sender of the previous message. The communication overhead of TESLA is minimal, especially since the keys are sent alongside the data of the next message. However, the unavoidable time delay between receiving and authenticating a message limits TESLA's applicability in real-time systems. Groza et al. [39] argue that this delay is too large for intra-vehicle communication scenarios. Furthermore, TESLA only supports limited receiver authentication in communication systems without sender identifiers, and does not provide stream authorization or encryption.

LiBra-CAN.   For the automotive domain, LiBra-CAN is presented in [39]. It authenticates senders at the receiving ECUs via Mixed Message Authentication Codess (M-MACs). Keys are assigned to groups of ECUs. LiBra-CAN requires pre-shared keys and does not concern itself with key exchanges.

CANAuth.   In [173], CANAuth, a very lightweight authentication mechanism, is proposed. CANAuth allows broadcast authentication and keys are assigned for message groups. Similar to LiBra-CAN, CANAuth requires pre-shared keys, before authentication can be performed for message groups.

VeCure.   More recently, VeCure has been proposed in [177]. VeCure splits ECUs into classes based on trust and assigns keys to these classes. However, VeCure also relies on pre-programmed keys and proposes to program these at the initial setup of the vehicle.

Most frameworks in literature rely on pre-programmed keys. However, such approaches are not realistic, sufficient or effective. The secure generation and the programming of keys is not discussed and not a trivial problem. Additionally, due to the long lifetime of vehicles, keys must be renewed regularly, to avoid attacks. Further, the exchange of ECUs in workshop situations is difficult or even impossible. Thus, the integration aspects are not considered here, making the protocols unsuitable for real-world applications.

Simulators. In literature, several simulators have been proposed for network analysis. The OPNET Modeler [141] is a modular simulation framework that enables protocol and network design for various scenarios, including CAN bus simulations [43]. The temporal behavior of automotive networks, including end-to-end latencies and data throughput, can be analyzed at the bit-level with OPNET. This is ideal for analyzing short sequences of network transmissions with high accuracy. However, longer-term network analysis, such as the setup of a secure communication architecture in a vehicle, is precluded by its performance limits. Thus, in this work, we focus on simulation on the message-level, while taking specified bit timings into account.

NS-2 [78] is a discrete-event simulator that implements numerous network protocols and is able to simulate traffic or routing in networks. It can be extended by user-defined protocol implementations and run various network architectures. Currently, no established support for automotive use cases and protocols exists and such architectures would need to be implemented from scratch, with effort close to that required to design In-Vehicle Network Simulator (IVNS).

OMNeT++ is an open-source discrete event simulation framework that provides tools to write and run simulations for any type of network [174]. It enables large-scale simulations, visualization of message flows, and can be extended with user-defined protocols and architectures. Internal automotive networks such as CAN or Ethernet can be analyzed and implemented by this framework [102]. However, implementing our proposed model into the rigid framework of OMNeT++, especially including the parametrization of the components, is cumbersome. Database lookups, as well as filtering, formatting, and exporting of results create additional hurdles. Thus, implementation in OMNeT++ would exceed the effort of implementing the model in a new environment. Once our model and approach are implemented, these can be combined into an OMNeT++ library in future work.

Other commercially available simulators are Timing Architects' Simulator [167], Symta Vision's SymTA/S & Trace Analyzer [163], and Inchron's ChronSIM [50]. While [167] is focused exclusively on the simulation of multi-core systems, [163] and [50] also support the simulation of networks. However, while these tools offer many interfaces for integration with existing workflows in the automotive industry, the libraries for simulating components and protocols are limited to those supplied by the manufacturer, and cannot easily be extended to enable prototyping of security measures. Neither offers security protocols.

Hardware Support. As an alternative to the hardware co-processors for encryption shown in Section 1.6.3, other approaches have integrated support for security functions into the network controller. An approach for this integration of encryption into standard network controllers has been proposed in [153]. There the implementation has been shown to have no impact on the communication latency. A fully featured implementation with symmetric cryptography and protocol obfuscation has been shown in [154]. These approaches rely on network controllers with additional functionality, implemented on Field Programmable Gate Arrays (FPGAs). Such an approach can augment the presented mechanisms, but is only suitable for large ECUs, which can integrate an FPGA.

4.3 Authentication & Authorization

In this section, we introduce the ECU authentication (Section 4.3.2) and stream authorization (Section 4.3.3) approaches in detail.

4.3.1 Terminology

The following terminology is used to describe the framework. We denote an ECU as e, sending a set of streams S_e to a set of receiving ECUs R_e. In turn, a stream $s \in S_e$ is identified by the sending ECU e, a set of receiving ECUs R_s and a set of message instances M_s: $s = (e, R_s, M_s)$. A message instance $m \in M_s$ is assigned to a stream s and carries a payload o. The security module of the system is denoted as y. A timestamp on device d is denoted as ω_d and a random number as ρ. A nonce n is a unique random number ρ within the accuracy of one timestamp. Together, a timestamp and nonce shall be unique over the lifetime of the vehicle, while minimizing the storage required for nonces. A key is denoted as k and identified by its value v and its length l. We further define a hashing function for message m on device d as $h_d(m)$. A parameter to determine if the system is running is defined as $\theta \in \{0, 1\}$ and a function $\alpha(e, s) \in \{0, 1\}$ determines if an ECU e has access to the stream s (1) or not (0). The time required to execute a function x is defined as τ_x. An action z is triggered, if a condition i is fulfilled: $i \rightarrow z$.

4.3.2 ECU Authentication

The key exchange used for ECU keys is based on the Public Key Cryptography for Initial Authentication in Kerberos (PKINIT) protocol for Kerberos. PKINIT has been chosen for its conciseness. This reduces the required time and bandwidth for the authentication. The ECU authentication is illustrated in Figure 4.2 and described in the following. This mechanism facilitates the initial key exchange between the ECU and the security module, and is based on asymmetric cryptography. Secure asymmetric cryptography is generally a computationally expensive task. This holds especially for software implementations without hardware support, as will be the case on most ECUs. Thus, this ECU authentication needs to be executed when the vehicle is not in use as not to interfere with the real-time capabilities of the system (see Section 4.4).

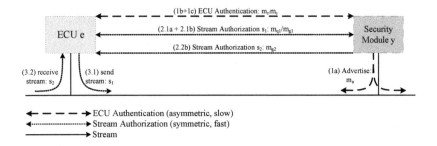

Figure 4.2: *In our framework, every ECU is authenticated against the security module (1a-1c). Subsequently, the ECU can request the keys for a message stream (2.1a-2.1b) and start transmitting (3.1). If the ECU is to start receiving a message stream, it is notified by the security module with the message stream key (2.2b) before it receives the stream (3.2).*

Authentication Mechanism. To describe ECU authentication, we define a set of keys for device d, consisting of a public key $k_{d,\text{pub}}$ and a private key $k_{d,\text{priv}}$. We further define an asymmetric encryption function ϵ^a for device d, that translates clear text t into cipher text c with key k, such that $c = \epsilon_d^a(t, k)$. Accordingly, we define an asymmetric decryption function δ^a for device d, that translates cipher text c into clear text t with key k, such that $t = \delta_d^a(c, k)$. For authentication, we further require the certificate f_d for device d and a function $\phi_{d_1}(f_{d_2}) = \{0, 1\}$ to verify the certificate f_{d_2} on device d_1.

As shown in Figure 4.2, three steps are required to authenticate an ECU. First, the security module needs to make itself known and authenticate to all ECUs. Second, each ECU authenticates to the security module and requests a symmetric key. Third, the security module permits the requesting ECU to access the bus by sending a confirmation message to this ECU. These steps are described in the following:

(a) Advertisement by the security module (Figure 4.2 (1a)): The security module y advertises its certificate to every ECU on the bus at startup with message m_a. This certificate is required to be signed by the appropriate Certificate Authority (CA) (see Section 4.4.1).

$$\theta \to m_a \text{ with } m_a \in M_s^a, \ s = (y, \{e\}, M_s^a), \ o = f_y \tag{4.1}$$

The authentication begins with the security module y presenting its security certificate f_y to ECU e. This certificate includes the security module's public key, and is broadcast on the network unencrypted. Each ECU has a list of trusted CAs, which it uses to verify the signature on the security module's certificate. This list of trusted CAs can be updated by the manufacturer using the remote software update procedure (see Section 4.4.5).

(b) Registration of the ECU (Figure 4.2 (1b)): Once the security module has been successfully authenticated ($\phi_e(f_y) = 1$), the ECU transmits its registration message m_r, including its own certificate f_e and the newly generated ECU key $k_{e,\text{sym}}$. The key, a timestamp ω_e and a nonce n are encrypted with the public key of the security module $k_{y,\text{pub}}$ and can thus only be decrypted by the security module. The certificate f_e contains the ECU's identity and public key, as well as any manufacturer-defined properties of the ECU (e.g. type of ECU, current software version):

$$\phi_e(f_y) \rightarrow m_r \tag{4.2}$$

with $m_r \in M_s^r$, $s = (e, \{y\}, M_s^r)$,

$$o = (\epsilon_e^a((e, y, k_{e,\text{sym}}, n, \omega_e), k_{y,\text{pub}}), \epsilon_e^a(h(e, y, k_{e,\text{sym}}, n, \omega_e), k_{e,\text{priv}}), f_e)$$

Note the term $\epsilon_e^a(h(e, y, k_{e,\text{sym}}, n, \omega_e), k_{e,\text{priv}})$. Though computationally expensive, this signature is required to securely identify the sender of the message.

(c) Confirmation of the security module (Figure 4.2 (1c)): Upon receiving the registration message, the security module authenticates the ECU by decrypting the received hash from m_r and comparing it to the hash of the received elements. The elements have been received separately in m_r and need to be decrypted with the private key of the security module $k_{y,\text{priv}}$. Additionally, the certificate of the sender is verified and, in the case of successful verification ($\phi_y(f_e) = 1$), the security module saves the ECU key, the ECU identity, and any manufacturer-defined information. The security module then sends a confirmation message m_c to the ECU. This message contains the ECU identifier encrypted with the newly exchanged symmetric ECU key:

$$\delta_y^a(\epsilon_e^a(h(y, k_{e,\text{sym}}, n, \omega_e), k_{e,\text{priv}}), k_{e,\text{pub}}) = h(y, k_{e,\text{sym}}, n, \omega_e)) \wedge \phi_y(f_e) \rightarrow m_c \tag{4.3}$$

with $m_c \in M_s^c$, $s = (y, \{e\}, M_s^c)$, $o = (e, y, \epsilon_y^s((e, n, \omega_y), k_{e,\text{sym}}))$

In addition to the certificate and signature verification steps described above, the validity of all timestamps is checked for every message.

In order to transmit messages via an encrypted channel, the ECU must request a stream key from the security module. This is handled via the stream authorization protocol, as described in the following.

4.3.3 Stream Authorization

After an ECU has authenticated itself to the security module and established a symmetric ECU key, the ECUs can request initiations of message streams. All message streams and stream keys in the system are managed by the security module. Each message stream uses a unique (within the network) stream key, which the sending and receiving ECUs request from the security module. By centralizing ECU authentication and stream authorization at the security module, our framework eliminates the need for the sending and receiving ECUs to authenticate each other. This reduces the number of messages and in turn latency in the protocol. The stream setup can be performed when a message stream is required, or, if the real-time requirements are more stringent than the stream setup time, considerably in advance (e.g. at vehicle start-up).

Authorization Mechanism. For stream authorization, we define a symmetric key k_{sym} and two functions ϵ^s and δ^s for encryption and decryption, such that $c = \epsilon_d^s(t, k_{\text{sym}})$ and $t = \delta_d^s(c, k_{\text{sym}})$ for plaintext t and ciphertext c on device d.

The stream can only be established after the ECU receives the confirmation message m_c from the ECU authentication protocol (see Figure 4.2 (1c)). The stream is usually established when a message m is requested to be sent. The sending ECU e requests a key from the security module y, allowing access to the stream. The request message m_q contains the identifier of the requested stream s_i, the identifier of the requesting ECU e, as well as a timestamp ω_e and a nonce n to protect against malicious retransmissions. The content of the message m_q is encrypted with the ECU key $k_{e,\text{sym}}$:

$$m_c \wedge m \to m_q \tag{4.4}$$
$$\text{with } m_q \in M_s^q, \ s = (e, \{y\}, M_s^q),$$
$$o = (e, \epsilon_e^s((e, s_i, n, \omega_e), k_{e,\text{sym}}))$$

If the received request message m_q can be successfully decrypted with the ECU key $k_{e,\text{sym}}$, it must have originated from the correct ECU. The security module can then make an access control decision based on the stored information about that particular ECU. The security module can support arbitrarily-complex access control policies defined by the manufacturer. One such policy could be for the security module to maintain an access control list (ACL) based on the ECU identities. If the security module determines that the requesting ECU e is allowed access to the stream s_i ($\alpha(e, s_i) = 1$), the security module y assigns a new stream key $k_{s_i,\text{sym}}$. This key is first sent to all receiving ECUs in the stream $\tilde{e} \in R_{s_i}$, and then to the requesting sending ECU e. In this way, the protocol ensures that all receivers have access to the data as soon as it is sent:

$$m_q \wedge (\delta_y^s(m_q, k_{e,\text{sym}}) = (e, s_i, \omega_e, n)) \tag{4.5}$$
$$\wedge (\omega_e \leq \omega_y) \wedge \alpha(e, s_i) \to \forall \tilde{e} \in \{R_{s_i}, e\} : m_g$$
$$\text{with } m_g \in M_s^g, \ s = (y, \tilde{e}, M_s^g),$$
$$o = \epsilon_y^s((\tilde{e}, s_i, k_{s1,\text{sym}}, n_i, \omega_y), k_{\tilde{e},\text{sym}}),$$
$$n_i = \rho : \rho \notin \bigcup_l \rho_l, l = \{0..i - 1\}$$

In theory, it would be possible to allow access to any ECU of the correct type (e.g. motor control) that presents a valid certificate. However, it must be assumed that some ECU keys may have been compromised by the adversary. Since it is not always possible to check the validity of a given certificate, using an ACL based on ECU type could lead to widespread attacks if the adversary extracts a key from a popular type of ECU (e.g. infotainment). The use of individual ECU identities in the ACL limits the scope of such an attack to a single vehicle (usually the adversary's own vehicle).

4.4 Integration

As for every security measure, the integration is an important factor to guarantee the security. In the following, we describe the handling of certificate validations, as well as scenarios outside the typical application of LASAN, such as the setup of the vehicle. These aspects are an essential part of every authentication framework to ensure full vehicle functionality. However, in literature, these aspects are often not covered, also because their implementation is not trivial, often leading to suboptimal implementations and security flaws.

4.4.1 Certificate Validation

The security of digital certificates depends on the security of the corresponding private keys. Any entity that knows the relevant private key can claim the identity and attributes described in the certificate. Therefore, if a private key is stolen or purposely distributed, the corresponding certificate can no longer be trusted. For example, if the private key of an ECU is stolen, a malicious device can impersonate that specific ECU to the rest of the vehicle network. Although ECU manufacturers can take measures to protect the private keys, it must be assumed that some private keys might be extracted from ECUs. In particular, an adversary with the right tools and physical access to an ECU (e.g. an after-market component) would likely be able to extract the private key. In light of this, our system is designed to minimize the impact of a compromised private key, as far as possible.

The same challenges regarding compromised private keys also arise on the Internet and in other traditional computer networks that make use of digital certificates. In those contexts, approaches such as Certificate Revocation Lists (CRLs) [17] and the Online Certificate Status Protocol (OCSP) [146] are used to address this issue. However, neither of these approaches is suitable for use in vehicular networks, due to the unique characteristics and constraints of this domain. CRLs are essentially lists of certificates that have been revoked (e.g., because of a known compromise of the private key). In order to be effective, CRLs must be frequently updated and checked whenever a certificate is verified. Although many modern vehicles are likely to have connectivity to external networks, it cannot be assumed that this connectivity will be available at all times (e.g., the vehicle may lose connectivity if traveling in a remote area). Furthermore, CRLs on the Internet usually contain a large number of revoked certificates, making it burdensome for the vehicle to frequently download these relatively large data sources and to store and process these lists when checking certificates. To avoid the need to download large CRLs, OCSP allows a verifier to query the status of an individual certificate, to ascertain whether or not it has been revoked. However, this requires always-on connectivity in order to check individual certificates, which again may not always be available. Furthermore, both of these techniques present the adversary with new vectors to mount denial of service attacks against the vehicle network. For example, if the adversary can change the OCSP response or cause the vehicle to download a modified CRL, the vehicle may refuse to accept certificates from legitimate ECUs. Although this may not be a serious issue on the Internet, this type of attack would have a much greater impact in the vehicle network context. A potential attack could be the disabling of the brake controller and thus the brakes at high-speeds.

Instead of using CRLs or OCSP, we have designed a new protocol specifically for use in vehicle network contexts. The main ideas behind our certificate validation protocol are as follows:

- The vehicle manufacturer should not be required to provide an online service (e.g. OCSP) since this may incur high operating costs, especially because it would have to be available for the full life of all vehicles on the road.

- The protocol does not attempt to prevent owners from intentionally installing modified/rogue ECUs in their own vehicles. However, in the event of an investigation, this should be detectable in order to ascertain liability in case of vehicle malfunction.

- The protocol only takes place when an ECU is added/exchanged, since this is when the system is most vulnerable.

- The validation step relies on a human-in-the-loop, who could either be the vehicle owner or a trusted representative (e.g. a vehicle workshop).

- The protocol must not restrict the choice of workshops/service centres at which the vehicle may be serviced, since this may be considered anti-competitive behaviour.

The full details of our certificate validation protocol are presented in the system life-cycle scenarios in the next section.

4.4.2   System Life-Cycle Scenarios

Throughout its lifetime, every vehicle experiences a certain set of scenarios, which are divergent from the standard driving behavior. It is essential for any authentication protocol targeted to the automotive domain to address these use cases. Thus, to ensure full operational capabilities, these situations must be handled in LASAN. In this section, we describe these scenarios, as well as the support by LASAN.

4.4.3   System Setup

The first non-standard situation the vehicle experiences is the manufacturing of its components and the assembly of the vehicle in the factory. This process is shown in Figure 4.3. At some

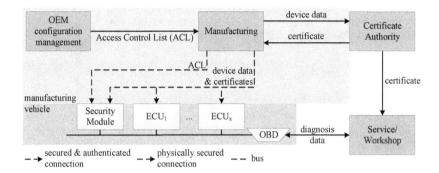

Figure 4.3: *Overview of system setup and workshop situations. At manufacturing, every device is programmed an ID and a certificate. Security modules are additionally supplied the Access Control List (ACL) for the vehicle. A workshop connects to the vehicle via a secured connection to the On-Board Diagnosis (OBD) port. All participants are certified by the central Certificate Authority (CA) of the Original Equipment Manufacturer (OEM).*

point in this process, the ECUs and security module are bare and do not have any security certificates or keys. The security of all devices and connections in the following process is essential to guarantee the security of subsequent states.

Where possible, the asymmetric key pairs are generated by the relevant devices (i.e. the security modules and ECUs). However, where this is not possible, these keys are generated externally and securely provisioned onto the devices. To facilitate the certificate validation protocol, each device is assigned a globally-unique human-readable ID (e.g. a short alpha-numeric code), which is printed on the physical device. Each device is issued a digital certificate that contains its device ID, its public key, and any device-specific information (e.g. type of device and operating parameters). This certificate is signed by the respective Certificate Authority (CA), which could be the device manufacturer. This certificate binds the device ID to its public key, and thus only a device in possession of the corresponding private key can assert that identity. During this process, the programming connection between computer and device must be secured both digitally and physically. This connection can be placed in the manufacturing process of the device, ideally at the first start of the device (ECU or security module).

As explained in the previous section, the security module holds an Access Control List (ACL) containing all permissible message streams. The IDs of the authorized sending and receiving ECUs for each stream are programmed into this ACL. With this list, the security module can verify if all ECUs are correctly built into the vehicle and which ECUs have access to which streams. The list can be automatically generated by the configuration management of the Original Equipment Manufacturer (OEM) and must be signed with the corresponding certificate. Note that an ACL is a feasible method here, as the distribution of tasks and messages is known at design time. In case this changes via a functionality update, this may also contain an update to the ACL.

4.4.4   Vehicle Service

Although a vehicle network may not change frequently, there will always be a need to replace certain components in the system. For example, this might happen when a damaged ECU needs to be replaced. To the best of our knowledge, LASAN is the only framework supporting such exchanges. In the following, we describe the protocol to exchange ECUs but omit message details for conciseness.

The two objectives of this protocol are (1) to determine whether or not a particular ECU is authentic and, (2) to securely add its ID to the ACL held by the security module.

The first objective is achieved using the ID printed on the physical device and makes use of manual validation as follows: When a new ECU is ready to be added, the vehicle owner or workshop attempts to determine whether the same ECU ID appears in any other vehicle. If it does, this means that there is more than one ECU with access to that particular private key, indicating that the key has been compromised. To facilitate the process of checking for duplicate IDs, vehicle owners and workshops should be encouraged to publish the lists of ECU IDs they have installed. These public lists can then be consulted to check for duplicate IDs. This process is similar to the concept of Certificate Transparency, recently developed and deployed by Google [90].

Once satisfied that the ECU is authentic, the vehicle's owner puts the vehicle into a special state in which new ECU IDs can be added to the security module's ACL. Various different approaches could be used to authenticate the owner and put the vehicle into this state, including a physical switch, a special vehicle key, an owner password, or a combination of these factors. Once in this state, the owner or workshop can add the ECU and verify that the digital ID matches the ID printed on the physical device.

It is a deliberate design decision that this procedure is not fully automated, and we argue that this level of manual intervention is both feasible and necessary, given that vehicle service is not likely to be a frequent occurrence. Since the vehicle owner authorizes this process, there is no need to contact the manufacturer. This also means that the owner may permit any third party to perform the vehicle service (e.g. the vehicle is not restricted to manufacturer-approved service stations). The security module keeps a record of the ECU IDs that have been added in this way, and this record can be audited if need be (e.g. as part of an investigation into vehicle malfunction).

4.4.5   Firmware updates

In connected vehicles, the possibility of Over-The-Air (OTA) updates is becoming increasingly important. For unconnected vehicles, firmware updates are usually performed at workshops. By being able to update software at any point in time, the number of visits to repair shops, as well as the downtime of the vehicle are reduced significantly. However, firmware updates, especially Over-The-Air (OTA) updates, can compromise security, if not handled properly. OTA updates are available in some vehicles on the market today. In these cases, signed firmware updates are used and are verified by the receiving ECU, if possible. If the receiving ECU does not have the computational power to verify the certificate, an additional element, such as the cellular gateway can perform this task. In this case, the programming of the ECU is performed over the internal networks without security, based on trust. The only security measure against illegitimate firmware updates from the Controller Area Network (CAN) bus is usually a simple password that can often be recovered from the tuner community [85].

In LASAN, we can replace this simple password with our authentication scheme and ensure that the firmware update is authenticated all the way to the ECU. All firmware updates are run via the security module, which in turn verifies the identity of the sender and the validity of the firmware signature for the ECU. The firmware is signed with the private key of the sending instance, which is certified by an appropriate CA (see Section 4.4.1). After successful validation, the security module triggers the programming of the ECU. To ensure a maximum of security, the ECU authentication (see Section 4.3.2), including the re-validation of the security module certificate, is started as soon as a reprogramming command is received and before a new firmware is accepted. After successful authentication of both the security module and the ECU, the update is installed on the ECU.

In this Section we presented an essential part of LASAN, the integration with the processes in the automotive domain. Although often omitted in literature, the protocols and considerations described are necessary requirements for any authentication framework design, as they represent the use cases which must be supported by the authentication framework.

4.5   Verification

In this Section, we focus on the modeling and security verification of the protocols contained in the framework with the protocol verification tool Scyther [18]. We provide a brief introduction to Scyther and define our adversary model. As it is not possible to verify the overall framework, we separately verify the protocols contained in LASAN. For this, we do require a set of assumptions, which we will detail here. We then present the formal models of the protocols and the results of the verification. As conceptual security is paramount in authentication frameworks, the models developed in the following will be made available online for public scrutiny.

Scyther Tool.   The Scyther tool, developed by Cremers [18, 19], performs automatic symbolic analysis of security protocols in terms of their confidentiality (secrecy) and authentication properties. In Scyther, protocols are modeled as sets of *role scripts* which are executed by *entities*. Each execution of a role is called a session and multiple concurrent sessions are permitted for any role. The desired security properties for a protocol are modeled as *claims* made by specific roles. If a claim is falsified, Scyther offers a counterexample showing the sequence of events leading to that point, which will usually represent a potential attack against the protocol. For certain claims, Scyther can perform *unbounded verification* which, if successful, indicates that the claim will not be falsified irrespective of how many times the protocol is run [19]. Internally, Scyther uses the concept of *patterns* to reason about infinite sets of traces in a protocol [19]. A pattern forms a labeled directed acyclic graph that, under certain conditions, could be a realization of the protocol under analysis. Patterns can be *refined* according to a set of rules and well-typed substitutions. The verification algorithm applies a pattern that violates a specific claim and attempts to refine this into a realizable pattern that then represents a counterexample to the claim.

Adversary Model.   In line with the majority of security protocol analyses, we assume a Dolev-Yao adversary model [24], in which the adversary has full control over all communication and is thus able to intercept, modify, replay or block any messages, as well as inject new constructed messages. This is appropriate for our application domain since the adversary could, for example, be a malicious device connected to the communication bus which, in the worst case, would be the central gateway, able to exert this degree of control over all messages on the bus. In the model, the adversary can also perform any role, which in practice means that the adversary could pretend to be any device on the bus. However, the Dolev-Yao adversary is assumed to be computationally bounded and thus unable to break cryptographic primitives (encryption, digital signatures, hash functions etc.) in a reasonable amount of time. This is a realistic assumption, given that these cryptographic primitives are widely used in other domains (including Internet communication) and are not known to be broken. Finally, it is always possible that a real-world adversary might be able to compromise one of the legitimate devices (e.g., through malicious software or runtime exploits). However, since this is almost entirely dependent on the actual hardware and software implementations, this class of attacks is beyond the scope of our analysis and we assume that an authenticated device is secure.

ECU Authentication.   The model of the ECU authentication protocol is described in Section 4.3.2. While the design of the framework includes the distribution of certificates in messages m_a (Equation (4.1)) and m_r (Equation (4.2)), these certificates are omitted in the Scyther model. The verification of certificates depends on external knowledge, such as locally available root certificates or connections to external verification agencies, such as the certificate CA. This exceeds the complexity that Scyther can verify and certificates are thus omitted in our analysis. As methods for initial certificate distribution and verification have been used successfully and securely for many years on the Internet, these can be applied here as well and the omission is reasonable.

To verify security, we define a set of claims which, if they hold, ensure the security of the protocol. This step is crucial, as insufficient claims would lead to security flaws being ignored by Scyther. Each role makes the following two security claims after the protocol:

1. Secrecy of symmetric ECU key: If neither the ECU's nor the security module's private keys have been compromised, then the newly established shared key cannot be known by the adversary. This is due to the fact that the only way to recover the shared key is by decrypting it with the private key of either component.

2. Non-injective synchronization: On completion of a protocol run, all entities agree on the roles that have been taken and the data items that have been exchanged. This synchronization is *non-injective* in the sense that replays of complete protocol runs are excluded since these would be detected using the nonces and timestamps in the messages.

Scyther confirms that both of these claims are successfully verified in the unbounded sense from both the perspective of the ECU and the security module. This means that under the defined Dolev-Yao adversary model, this protocol ensures the confidentiality of the newly-generated shared key and achieves mutual authentication.

Stream Authorization. The model of the stream authorization protocol described in Section 4.3.3.

While in reality, streams can be received by more than one ECU, it is sufficient to verify the protocol with two participants, as this covers all messages transmitted. In the case of an additional receiver, a duplicate message is added in the system, which does not affect the security.

The security module communicates with each ECU using the unique ECU key, kesym, established in the ECU authentication protocol. In this model, we assume that all ECU keys have been securely established and use Scyther's built-in pairwise keys (e.g. k(E1, SM)) to represent ECU keys. This is required to simplify the protocol representation and separately verify the ECU authentication and stream authorization. Having access to the stream key implicitly authorizes an ECU to participate in that stream and no further authentication is performed in order to minimize the communication latency.

All authorization decisions are made by the security module but these are orthogonal to the security claims of the communication protocol and are therefore beyond the scope of this model (see Section 4.4.3). The access to a stream is defined at design time by the system designer and is programmed into the security module, together with the certificates. In this model, neither the sending nor receiving ECUs make security claims because they do not have control or visibility over which other ECUs receive the stream key. The stream key is distributed by the security model and can thus not be assumed as secret by a single ECU. These ECUs, therefore trust the security module to distribute the stream key correctly. The influence of this on the security of the protocol is discussed in Section 4.7.3

The security module, which has overall visibility of the system, makes the following claims:

1. Secrecy of stream key: If none of the ECU keys have been compromised, then the newly established stream key cannot be known by the adversary. As the stream key is transmitted in messages encrypted with the ECU key, this sets up a chain between ECU and stream key.

2. Non-injective synchronization: On completion of a protocol run, all entities agree on the roles that have been taken and the data items that have been exchanged. Just as in the ECU authentication, this synchronization is *non-injective* as replays could be detected based on the message nonces and timestamps.

We modeled the protocol in the proprietary language required by Scyther and defined the claims above. Feeding this input to Scyther, it confirms that both of these claims are successfully verified in the unbounded sense. This means that under the Dolev-Yao adversary model, this protocol ensures that the stream key is only known to the set of ECUs determined by the security module's authorization policy, thus authorizing these ECUs to participate in the message stream.

In this section, we successfully verified the security of the protocols in the lightweight authentication framework. With the security being proven by a model checker, we now advance to evaluate the performance of the lightweight authentication framework with a discrete event simulation.

4.6   Simulation

For the evaluation of LASAN, we developed IVNS, a discrete event simulation of vehicular networks, implementing our protocol. We use this simulation to evaluate the performance of the lightweight authentication framework by implementing a set of synthetic test cases. This section describes the underlying model and the implementation of the simulator.

4.6.1   Model

In the following, we describe the formal model of the simulator and the simulation environment. The model is required to represent a security-enabled automotive architecture, as well as the configuration and calibration of the simulation. While the architecture A under test is the target of any analysis, the configuration C defines the basic configuration of the system and simulator, such as the used cryptographic algorithms and validity parameters. The calibration, in turn, is based on benchmarks P created on real-world systems, thus tuning the components of the architecture to represent existing hardware. Furthermore, the model can be validated through comparison with real-world systems, based on the set of parameters used for calibration and

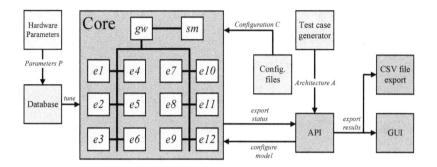

Figure 4.4: *Architecture of the simulator with a 12 cell setup on a single bus. The IVNS includes a test case generator generating architecture A, database of hardware parameters P, configuration files C, as well as GUI and CSV output via an API.*

obtained from the same hardware. We follow a compositional approach, combining these basic simulation components to represent the complete system behavior.

The IVNS defines a simulation s which contains the architecture A to be evaluated, the configuration C, as well as a set of parameters P, depicted in Figure 4.4:

$$s = (A, C, P) \tag{4.6}$$

Architecture. The architecture A contains the set of ECUs E, buses B, and gateways G, as well as their interconnections I:

$$A = (E, B, G, I) \tag{4.7}$$

A small subsystem is shown in Figure 4.5.

An ECU $e \in E$ is identified by its application a, one or multiple communication modules $mc \in MC$ and its hardware implementation HW:

$$e = (a, MC, HW) \tag{4.8}$$

The hardware components HW define the latencies t induced in every communication module mc. These components are the central processor μ, one or multiple communication controllers $o \in O$, as well as one or multiple transceivers $tr \in T$ generating the physical signals. Furthermore, an ECU might contain a hardware accelerator acc for cryptographic operations:

$$HW = (\mu, O, T, acc) \tag{4.9}$$

Each application a running on an ECU e sends a set of messages $m \in M$. All messages with the same message identifier id are called a stream M_{id}. Each message m in such a stream

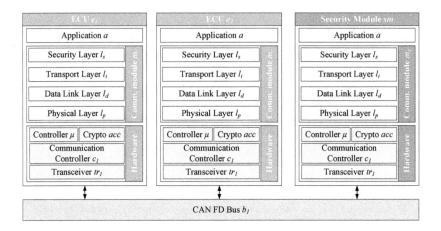

Figure 4.5: *A small subsystem with two ECUs (e_1, e_2), security module (sm) and CAN FD bus (b_1), including internal representation of ECUs and security module. The CAN FD transmission has been extended by a transport layer l_t, implementing segmentation according to ISO-TP (ISO 15765-2) and a security layer l_s, combining session (authentication) and presentation layer (encryption).*

M_{id} is called a message instance, or message. A message instance m can be secured by a function $sec(m)$. A stream needs to be authorized by a function $auz(M_{id})$. Depending on the security settings of the simulation, function $auz(M_{id})$ may trigger a set of authentication and/or authorization functions. In LASAN, e.g., an authentication $auc(e)$ is performed per ECU, after which message streams may be authorized.

The number of communication modules $mc \in MC$ depends on the number of controllers and transceivers available and used by the ECU. A communication module mc may contain all or a subset of layers as defined in the Open Systems Interconnect (OSI) model. This includes an application layer l_a, a presentation layer l_{pr}, a session layer l_{se}, a transport layer l_t, a network layer l_n, a data link layer l_d and a physical layer l_p:

$$mc = (l_a, l_{pr}, l_{se}, l_t, l_n, l_d, l_p) \tag{4.10}$$

Many bus systems require only a subset of these or summarize cross-layer functions. In CAN Flexible Data-Rate (FD) with segmentation according to ISO 15765-2, e.g., only transport layer l_t, data link layer l_d, and physical layer l_p are used. Furthermore, cross-layer security functions of session and presentation layer can be summarized as a security layer l_s. Cryptographic operations such as encryption/decryption and signing/verification are located in this security layer l_s. The security layer further handles stream initiation and authentication frameworks such as LASAN and TESLA.

Some authentication frameworks, such as LASAN, require a root of trust in the network. Being an ECU with defined security functions, a security module $sm \in E$ is defined as an ECU. The same holds for a gateway $gw \in G$, which is a type of ECU ($G \subset E$) with multiple interfaces where the application layer is filtering and forwarding messages depending on an ACL:

$$sm = gw = (a, MC, HW) \tag{4.11}$$

A bus $b \in B$ is defined by its properties, including data rate d, maximum message length l_{max}, bus access scheme mac, and the velocity factor v_P of the medium:

$$b = (d, l_{max}, mac, v_P) \tag{4.12}$$

Configuration. The configuration C contains the settings c valid for all components. This configuration defines the framework of the simulation, including the parameters such as key lengths and selected algorithm for encryption/decryption, signing/verification and hashing algorithms on ECUs, as well as other settings, such as the validity of nonces and certificates and maximum simulation times. The settings are dependent on the implemented layers and protocols, which can define and load any configuration setting and can thus be extended easily.

$$C = (alg_{sym}, keylen_{sym}, alg_{asym}, keylen_{asym}, alg_{hash}) \tag{4.13}$$

Other possible settings could be different operating modes for the security frameworks, caches or components, such as gateways.

Parameters. The parameters $p \in P$ are used to calibrate the IVNS to a real-world environment. Calibration parameters are typically obtained by benchmarking existing hardware. The calibration is crucial to be able to simulate reality as accurately as possible. Furthermore, this allows validation of the model and simulator through comparison of a calibrated simulation with the underlying hardware used for calibration. The required measurements depend on the selected algorithms but typically include cryptographic parameters, such as encryption/decryption, signing/verification, hashing, key generation, as well as transmission related parameters, such as gateway latencies and bit transmission times for the selected buses.

$$P = (t_{enc}, t_{dec}, t_{sign}, t_{verif}, t_{hash}, t_{GW}, t_{tx}) \tag{4.14}$$

Parameters can be defined as constants (e.g., bit timing on bus), lookup tables (e.g., encryption/decryption latencies) or functions (e.g., hashing latency). The parameters are loaded at runtime, based on the configuration of the individual components depending on these parameters. Furthermore, they are applied per ECU and can thus be used to define varying hardware for ECUs of different computational capabilities.

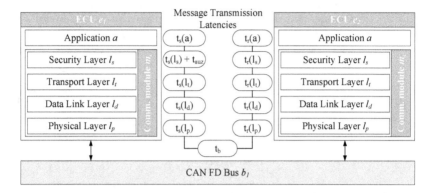

Figure 4.6: *Components of message transmission latencies per layer, as defined in our model. Function t_s defines the sending time, function t_r defines the receiving time, per layer, respectively. Depending on the security setup of the system, the security layer has high and varying influence on the message transmission latency, being responsible for encryption, as well as authentication and authorization.*

Message Flow. The components described above determine the latencies a message experiences when being sent. Every component and every layer defines and adds its own latencies. A simple message transmission is shown in Figure 4.6.

A message thus experiences the following delay t_m in conventional transmission, where t_s, t_b and t_r are sending, bus and receiving delays, respectively:

$$t_m = t_s + t_b + t_r \tag{4.15}$$

These components can be defined in more detail based on the layers (see Figure 4.6). On the sending ECU, a message experiences a delay t_s, which consists of the sending delays of the application $t_s(a)$, the security layer $t_s(l_s)$, the transport layer $t_s(l_t)$, the data link layer $t_s(l_d)$ and the physical layer $t_s(l_p)$:

$$t_s = t_s(a) + t_s(l_s) + t_s(l_t) + t_s(l_d) + t_s(l_p) \tag{4.16}$$

The bus introduces latency t_b, mostly depending on the data rate of the bus and the size of the message, as well as the velocity factor. On the receiving ECU, the message experiences a further latency t_r, consisting of the receiving latencies of the physical layer $t_r(l_p)$, the data link layer $t_r(l_d)$, the transport layer $t_r(l_t)$, the security layer $t_r(l_s)$ and the application $t_r(a)$:

$$t_r = t_r(l_p) + t_r(l_d) + t_r(l_t) + t_r(l_s) + t_r(a) \tag{4.17}$$

In case an authentication protocol is used, the first message might experience a longer sending delay t_a, as first, the authentication and authorization need to be performed. In this case

$$t_a = t_{auz} + t_s + t_b + t_r, \tag{4.18}$$

where t_{auz} is highly dependent on the authentication and authorization framework and the state of the system, specifically the number and size of messages required, as well as the selected authentication mechanisms and their speed on the ECU.

Protocols. The above latencies are the abstraction level of events for a discrete event simulation on the basis of OSI layers. The latencies per layer l are required to be calculated at runtime, based on the chosen implementation (e.g., CAN FD), required algorithms (e.g., encryption), state of the system (e.g., bus load) and inputs (e.g., message length), among others. Thus, the implementation needs to take into account the behavior of the layer l as defined in its specification, as well as the measurements of basic hardware parameters, as defined in the parameters P. The accuracy of the abstraction is defined through the detail of implementation. The runtime values might vary considerably, based on, e.g., bus access for t_b or, in case of LASAN, a potential authentication required before authorization, triggering a separate set of message transmissions. To achieve higher performance, these sub-layer latencies are computed at runtime and abstracted to a single event in the model, reducing the number of events considerably and thus increasing computational performance.

Modularity. The complexity of the model pays off when attempting to compare different networks. All components have defined functions, settings and interfaces. This allows a high amount of modularity in the system, as every component can be exchanged as required. For example, to exchange a bus system, only the implementation of the bus b needs to be adjusted. In the same manner, the authentication and authorization framework can be exchanged by changing the security layer l_s. Furthermore, the underlying hardware for an ECU e or the security module sm can be easily exchanged, simply by switching the parameter set P. In this way, it is easily possible to, e.g., add a cryptographic accelerator to an existing architecture.

Alternatively, single ECUs may be configured with a different set of parameters, only applicable to a specific ECU. This allows creation of different ECUs, some more powerful than others. While the base ECU of the architecture could be an 8-bit controller, e.g., used for the outer mirror of a car, some ECUs, such as the infotainment unit, might be significantly more powerful.

Granularity. This model represents the basic setup of an automotive architecture, including security components. The key to performance in the development of a simulation model is the abstraction level. Too detailed a model may result in unreasonably long computation times, while too highly abstracted a model results in insufficient accuracy of results.

We chose the abstraction level of our model to be especially efficient for the analysis of long-term processes in automotive systems, such as protocol analysis. To achieve this, we do not model single bit times as separate events, but summarize a set of latencies calculated at runtime into a single event in our discrete event simulation. The chosen abstraction for our model is on the level of OSI layers. We separately model the layers as events, but base the timeouts on the

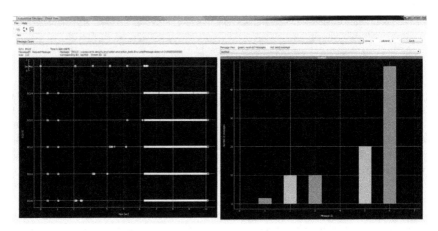

Figure 4.7: *A screenshot of the GUI. Here, a LASAN setup is shown. The Event View (left) shows every message sent and received on all buses. Red markers indicate the authentication of ECUs, green markers indicate the authorization of streams, and blue markers indicate data messages, occurring with significantly higher frequency after all streams have been set up securely. The Message View (right) shows the number of messages sent (red) or received (green) by a device, in this case the Security Module.*

parameter set P. This allows us to calculate latencies in the system with the accuracy of the smallest measurable time component, typically 1 bit time on the bus. However, due to bit times being summarized in events per layer, these smallest latencies cannot be exported or analyzed individually. Therefore, The smallest level for analysis is an OSI layer latency.

4.6.2 Implementation

The simulation framework implements the model as described in Section 4.6.1. The Python language has been used for implementation. Using an interpreted language like Python allows fast and easy extension of components. Furthermore, a large number of libraries are available, speeding up the implementation process, and simplifying future extension by the community. The discrete event handling is based on the Python library SimPy [164]. An overview of the components of the IVNS is given in Figure 4.4.

The simulation environment is set up with the given configuration C, typically read from configuration files. The network architecture A is either defined by the user, or generated by a test case generator and fed into the core of the simulation environment. The test case generator uses statistical processes to generate new architectures, based on a set of parameters for the architecture. These parameters include the number of ECUs, number of messages, etc. This architecture is calibrated by the parameters P, taken from hardware benchmarks. In our case, these benchmarks have been performed on an STM32F415 microcontroller for software and hardware implementations of cryptographic functions. These benchmarks will be published together with the IVNS for free use.

The Graphical User Interface (GUI) supports different plugins for analysis of the running system. A screenshot of the Event View and Message View is shown in Figure 4.7. There, the setup and operation of a system with the LASAN authentication framework, 5 ECUs and one security module are shown.

Every component in this simulation is built in a modular fashion and is easily exchangeable. A reporting and filtering system is in place, allowing collection, display, and export of any value in any of the components. These values could include the state of the ECU and security module buffers, the load on the bus, or the internal state of any task on an ECU. Reported values can be filtered to maximize performance of the IVNS and minimize the storage required for export files.

The IVNS has been built from the ground up with parametrization in mind. This allows easy import of externally generated parameters, e.g., latencies for encryption/decryption operations or the forwarding latency in a gateway, making the IVNS highly flexible. Initially, all implemented ECUs are based on an STM32 controller, but by adding parameters P measured on other devices, the IVNS can flexibly simulate any automotive networking environment.

4.7 Evaluation

In this section, we evaluate the performance of the IVNS proposed in the previous section with a set of synthetic test cases and a realistic case study. Furthermore, we analyze and evaluate the characteristics and performance of LASAN.

4.7.1 Simulator

We evaluate IVNS from multiple perspectives. On the one hand, we analyze the computation time and memory required for network systems of varying size and varying security protocols, to prove its performance. On the other hand, we demonstrate with a case study of a distributed battery management system how IVNS can be used to feed back performance data to the architecture design process. All computations in this section have been executed on an Intel Core i5-3450 CPU with 4 GB of RAM.

Synthetic Test Cases. To evaluate the computational and memory performance of IVNS, we implement two authentication protocols, LASAN and TESLA. Using the built-in test case generator (see Figure 4.4), we automatically generate architectures of varying sizes. These architectures include a varying number of ECUs and 500 messages. The number of receivers per message increases with the number of ECUs. This demonstrates the multicast behavior of messages in automotive networks.

The results are shown in Figure 4.8. As it can be clearly seen, the average memory requirement for a TESLA simulation stays fairly constant below 250 MB, even for large systems with up to 100 ECUs. The average memory usage for a LASAN simulation increases linearly, resulting from the larger number of messages transmitted in the system and needing to be stored in buffers. However, even for 100 ECUs, the memory requirement is less than half that of a TESLA simulation. As the number of receivers increases, the number of message objects to be processed in the separate receiving ECUs also increases. The higher memory requirement of the TESLA simulation originates from the number of keys being stored for all messages in the system. Here, we generate a chain of 400,000 keys, which is stored on the ECUs and applied in reverse order. This number is reasonable, as for a message with a period of 10 milliseconds, this set of keys lasts about 1 hour. In any case, the memory consumption for simulation of systems of realistic size stays below 250 MB, which is very low for modern desktop computers.

When evaluating the computation time required to simulate a network, we see a clear correlation between LASAN and TESLA in our simulator. This is expected, as both systems follow the same ECU- and bus-internal message sending sequences, as defined in Section 4.6.1. Though the computation time exhibits exponential behavior, even for large systems, it remains below 10 minutes. As in the automotive domain systems rarely exceed the threshold of 100 participants on the bus, this computation time is reasonable.

As all computations have been performed on a commercial off-the-shelf desktop computer, IVNS is ideal for evaluating automotive networks in a design environment. There, the feedback of the simulator can be used as an input to the optimization functions of other tools, or, as will be shown in the following case study, as feedback to the designer.

In summary, IVNS can be used to efficiently analyze automotive architectures of different sizes on commercial desktop computers, enabling designers to ensure real-time requirements while prototyping secure applications and security protocols. In the case of LASAN vs. TESLA, e.g., our simulator shows that LASAN allows setup of streams significantly more efficiently than TESLA, with stream setup times faster than 2 ms, on ECUs with cryptographic hardware accelerators. Details of this comparison will be shown in Section 4.7.2.

Case Study.   To show the applicability of IVNS to real-world applications, we analyze the case study of a distributed embedded Battery Management System (BMS), as might be used in next-generation Electric Vehicle (EV) batteries [161]. In this system, each cell in a battery is equipped with a microcontroller, allowing it to survey its own state of charge (SOC) and State of Health (SOH). Furthermore, such a setup can allow battery cells to exchange charge and thus implements active cell balancing in a distributed fashion. Secure communication is of particular importance in the context of such BMSs to ensure the safety of high-energy Lithium-Ion (Li-Ion) cells.

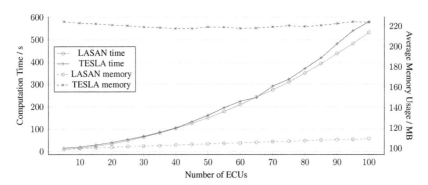

Figure 4.8: *Evaluation of computation time and average memory consumption of the simulator for architectures of different size and different authentication frameworks. IVNS stays below 10 minutes of computation time and below 250 MB of RAM for any realistic test case.*

In the following, we analyze the distributed battery management with and without cryptographic hardware acceleration, as well as for different numbers of cells and network topologies. The system is secured with the authentication framework LASAN. Different numbers of cells are used in different applications. Starting from 3 battery cells, such as for laptops, we increase the architecture size to 24 and 48 cells, often in use for electric bicycles and hybrid electric vehicles, respectively, up to 96 cells, such as in use for EVs. The architecture choice we investigate is the division of cells onto buses and has a large influence on complexity, weight and cost of the system. The number of buses, and a gateway, if required, cause additional weight and cost. On the other hand, connecting all battery cells to a single bus can lead to an increased bus load and thus system setup time, as all cells have to negotiate secure messages. The results are shown in Figure 4.9, illustrating the worst-case system setup time, representing authentication and authorization over the number of battery cells in the system. To estimate the worst-case setup time of the system, we assume that all battery cells need to transmit all status messages and charge exchange requests at the same time, right at the start of the system. While this is not a realistic test case (typically such transmissions are spread over a range of hours), it gives us a worst-case estimate for the setup time.

Evaluation. From Figure 4.9, we see that the hardware-accelerated system is significantly faster than the software-only implementations in all cases. This behavior is expected. The system setup time exhibits an exponential behavior, increasing with the number of cells in the system. This is due to the fact that the employed distributed battery management system uses broadcasts on nearly all messages. To achieve full security across all these messages and nodes, LASAN needs to exchange grant messages and cryptographic keys with every receiving ECU for every message to be sent.

In the case of large systems on a single bus, such as batteries for electric vehicles with 96 cells, hardware accelerated, as well as software only implementations, exhibit a very high latency of about 50 to 80 seconds.

Based on the behavior of LASAN and the requirements of the system, a designer might want to split the system into multiple buses. While this should decrease the setup time, quantifying the latency advantage is not trivial, due to it being based on the number of messages in the system and the number of receivers per message, as well as the performance of all ECUs. With IVNS, the system can easily be split into buses of different sizes. Results of these tests are also shown in Figure 4.9 for 12 and 24 cells per bus and hardware accelerated, as well as software-only implementations, respectively. As this split onto multiple buses leads to a large amount of parallelization across buses, the worst-case system setup time can be reduced significantly. In case of an electric vehicle battery with 96 cells and 12 cells per bus, the system setup time can be reduced to below 10 seconds. As for other systems the exponential behavior does not have such a large influence, the savings are smaller, yet significant. In the case of 48 cells, a typical hybrid electric vehicle battery, e.g., the setup time can be reduced from over 20 seconds to about 3 seconds, when using 12 cells per bus.

Optimization. These results can be be fed back into the architecture design. In case the specification, e.g., for an electric vehicle battery requires the designer to build a system with a worst-case system setup time of below 10 seconds, the results obtained by our simulator suggest a system with a maximum of 12 battery cells per bus and hardware acceleration. For the designer of an electric bike with 24 cells and similar requirements, the simulator clearly shows that the additional cabling effort and cost for hardware accelerated controllers required for a splitting of buses does not lead to much shorter setup times. In this context, the IVNS can be integrated with the design for secure communication architectures in vehicles.

This concludes the evaluation of IVNS. In the following, we will evaluate the proposed LASAN for security, as well as for performance, using IVNS.

4.7.2   LASAN

In the following, we will evaluate our authentication framework LASAN. For our tests, we are interested in the setup process of message streams and thus do not require a functional verification of the data itself. Therefore, we do not implement actual control algorithms, but transmit dummy data. However, the selected message size and timing patterns follow existing distributions.

We base our communication on a CAN FD bus [76]. CAN FD is an extension of CAN, allowing to increase the data rate in the data portion of the frame, such that a higher overall throughput can be achieved. Due to its low cost, similar to CAN, and backwards compatibility, CAN FD is likely to find widespread use in future networks.

The hardware parameters for the IVNS have been obtained from an STM32F415 microcontroller. In the context of automotive ECUs, this microcontroller is a midrange device and offers

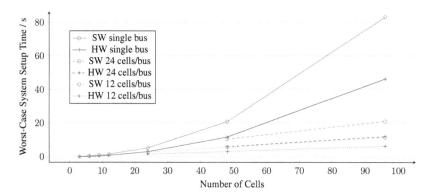

Figure 4.9: *Case study of a distributed embedded battery management system with the LASAN authentication framework. The worst-case system setup time has been analyzed for different systems with (HW) and without (SW) cryptographic hardware accelerators. Furthermore, the impact of the module size, or cells per bus on the setup time, is evaluated.*

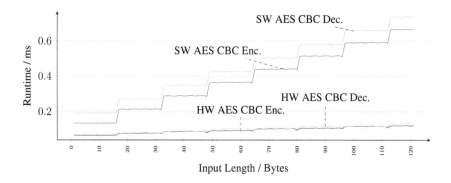

Figure 4.10: *AES performance for software implementations (SW) and with hardware support (HW). The measurements of encryptions (Enc.) and decryptions (Dec.) have been performed on an STM32 microcontroller with AES in Cipher Block Chaining (AES CBC) mode.*

key length (Bits)	public key operations	private key operations
512	0.206s	0.886s
1024	0.709s	4.977s
2048	2.626s	33.181s

Table 4.1: *Latencies of RSA encryption and decryption in software for different RSA key lengths, measured on an STM32F415 microcontroller.*

hardware acceleration for Advanced Encryption Standard (AES) encryption. Examples for the performance with AES with and without hardware acceleration are given in Figure 4.10. There, the encryption and decryption latencies depending on the clear text length are shown. Clearly visible are the block size of 128 Bit for AES in Figure 4.10.

The asymmetric RSA algorithm can only be implemented in software on this device, as no hardware acceleration exists. The encryption and decryption times depend on the key length. Examples are given in Table 4.1. Note the very long encryption and decryption times.

The authentication frameworks presented here are implemented transparently to the application layer. All handshakes and required messages are handled on the communication layers. From the perspective of the application layer, the start time of the network is simply increased.

All results shown in this work have been generated with the IVNS. For the results displayed here, we built three different communication layers for evaluation. These include LASAN as proposed in this work, as well as the existing authentication frameworks TLS and TESLA. TLS is mostly used in Internet traffic, e.g. in HTTPS connections. While not targeted for embedded systems or multicast communication, we implemented and used TLS v1.2 as a baseline [23]. We further implemented a communication layer utilizing TESLA [133] to compare with the other approaches. Both, TLS and TESLA have been implemented as timing correct. That means that not all functionality is fully implemented, but the correct lengths of cryptographic algorithm runtimes, message lengths and transmission times are ensured. On the other hand, to save memory and computational requirements for the simulator, identical certificates and keys are used for all ECUs. This is a reasonable approximation, as we are only interested in timing and not actual functionality of the protocols.

4.7.3   Security Comparison

Comparing the security of different approaches is no trivial task. Security flaws are often found based on implementation flaws, not conceptual flaws. As we are comparing the conceptual approaches, we keep the security comparison at a high level. In the following, we will shortly detail the cryptographic algorithms used in the different approaches and explain differences in the security.

To level the playing field and allow equal conditions for all compared frameworks, we use the same cryptographic methods for all approaches. For asymmetric functions, we use RSA with a key length of 512 Bits and an exponent of 65537. We use MD5 for hashing algorithm for the certificate calculations. For symmetric encryption, we use 128 Bit AES in the Cipher Block Chaining (CBC) mode.

We further assume that all keys used in the system have a limited security lifetime and must be renewed regularly. This is typically the case, as long key lifetimes increase the chances of reverse engineering via brute force attacks. It is necessary to exchange a key often enough that it is unlikely that a key can be brute forced within the given time. Note that multiple message transmissions with the same key do not have any influence on the security of the key, but the potential insecurity is a result of a key's long validity. Further, this time for brute force attacks decreases over time, as computational power increases, following Moore's Law.

Note that the TESLA Request For Comments (RFC) in [133] defines the message security mechanism to be used as MAC. The RFC does not consider encryption of messages. While this is sufficient to protect the integrity of messages (i.e. no attacker can alter or create a message without detection), the confidentiality (i.e. an attacker can read a message) remains unprotected. From the technical perspective, TESLA could also use exchanged keys for encryption, but the RFC only defines MACs and a strict implementation would need to follow this. While this does not impact the security of the authentication and authorization mechanisms, it does heavily impact the security of data messages.

TESLA further relies on a master key, securely exchanged before the conversation. This exchange is not further defined in the RFC [133] and it is suggested to use existing mechanisms. We assume here, similar to the other mechanisms, an initial key exchange via an asymmetric encryption scheme.

Furthermore, note that TLS only supports unicast messages. This increases the security, as no keys are shared among any of the participants, but also increases setup time, as a separate key needs to be exchanged with every receiver, as well as bus load, as duplicate messages need to be send for every receiver.

With LASAN, the symmetric message stream key is shared among all senders and receivers. As symmetric cryptography is used to protect message transmissions, it would be possible for a malicious receiver that has circumvented the ECU authentication and stream authorization to pretend to be the sender of a message stream and send message to all participants. This is however, easily detectable on the approved sender side, as a message is received that should never have existed on the bus. In this case, the current stream key can be voided and the communication participants (and possibly the user) can be notified of a breach in security. It would be possible to enhance LASAN with either a reverse key chain and include a MAC, such as in TESLA or use asymmetric signatures to enforce directionality in the message transmission. However, as we will show in Section 4.7.4, these approaches lead to significantly longer and unacceptable message transmission times. As this illicit behavior is easy to detect on the sender side, we do not require these additional measures.

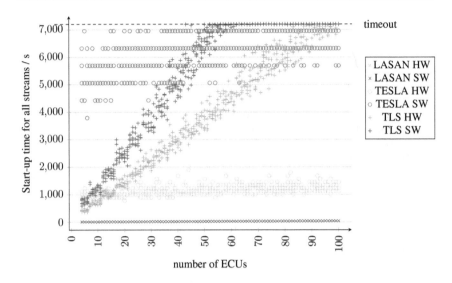

Figure 4.11: Comparison of start-up times in vehicles with varying numbers of ECUs and with different authentication frameworks (LASAN, TLS, TESLA) in software (SW) and hardware supported (HW) implementations. Architectures under test have been automatically generated and per number of ECUs, 5 test cases have been executed. Note that LASAN HW and SW are superimposed due to scale.

In summary, we can say that while there are slight differences in the concepts of the different approaches, the security of the authentication and authorization protocols should be comparable.

4.7.4   Latency Comparison

To evaluate the lightweight authentication framework, we use sets of randomly generated test-cases from our simulator. Based on the number of ECUs in the system, an architecture is generated. In this architecture, ECUs are assigned randomly to buses, if more than one bus is used, a central gateway is added. Messages are assigned random lengths and periods, based on real-world distributions and are distributed to the sending ECUs. To approach realistic network sizes, for every ECU in the network, five messages are assumed. Receiving ECUs are randomly assigned. Assignments of sending and receiving ECUs are controlled by setting a guiding Median Absolute Deviation (MAD) for the stream to ECU distribution.

We compare LASAN with the existing authentication frameworks TLS and TESLA. The results for a vehicle start-up without any previous authentication or authorization of any component or message are shown in Figure 4.11. There, we compare the worst-case startup-time, i.e. the time until all ECUs are authenticated and all messages are requested and authorized at the same time, for different numbers of ECUs and messages in the system. Both hardware- and software-supported implementations of the authentication frameworks are shown. In the following, we evaluate and interpret these results.

TLS. Clearly visible is the rapid latency increase for TLS with the number of ECUs and hence messages. As in TLS there is no common root of trust for message streams in the network, every message needs separate authentication between the sending ECU and all receiving ECUs. The overall start-up time is thus defined by the ECU sending or receiving most streams and thus requiring the longest time for encryption and decryption operations. Even at medium size networks of 40 ECUs onwards, the time for a full vehicle setup is in the range of one hour. For slightly larger networks of around 50 ECUs, start-up time reaches the simulation timeout of two hours.

TESLA. For TESLA, the structure of the protocol is visible in the form of delays in the key generation. As TESLA requires keys to be generated before transmissions, the number of key sets to be generated depends on the number of streams to be sent by one ECU. The slowest ECU, i.e. the ECU with the most streams to send, defines the start-up time of the vehicle. This key generation is visible as steps in Figure 4.11. In our testcases the number of messages sent by every ECU is kept relatively constant, based on a given MAD of 0.2. This is represented by the limited number of steps in Figure 4.11. The key generation needs to be performed periodically. In this setup, we are using 400,000 keys. Once these keys are exhausted, a new set needs to be generated. The period for key renewal is dependent on the period of the message, as for every transmission a single key is used. A set of 400,000 keys and a message period of 10ms requires a new set of keys to be generated after about 1h. With the number of ECUs and message streams in the network increasing, more often than not, a single ECU sends a larger set of messages.

Figure 4.11 clearly shows that hardware accelerated implementations of all authentication frameworks are significantly faster due to the faster encryption (compare Figure 4.10).

It is also clearly visible that TESLA and TLS have not been designed for the automotive environment, requiring real-time constraints and support for messages with multiple receivers. The key authentication (TLS) and preparation (TESLA) are far too large to be employed efficiently.

LASAN. Compared to TLS and TESLA, LASAN is significantly faster. By minimizing the number of message transmissions and the sizes of messages in the authentication and authorization process, we reduced the start-up time to a minimum. As shown in Figure 4.11, LASAN is faster for all realistic network sizes, i.e. from 20 ECUs onwards, even if only a software implementation is used.

LASAN is analyzed in more detail in Figure 4.12. There, a comparison of hardware and software implementations of the stream authorization is shown. The setup latency as depicted

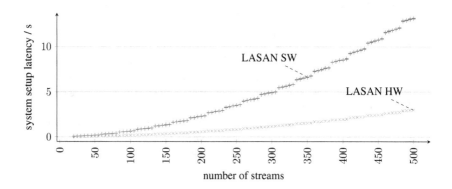

Figure 4.12: *Comparison of setup latencies for stream authorization in LASAN with software (SW) and hardware supported (HW) implementations over differing numbers of message streams.*

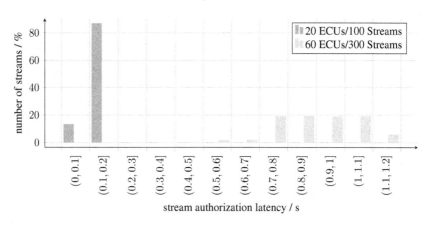

Figure 4.13: *Comparison of individual stream authorization times for architectures with 20 ECUs/100 Streams and 60 ECUs/300 Streams.*

here is the worst-case start-up time of the car, if all messages in the vehicle are authorized at the same time. This scenario is rather unlikely, as event-based messages without real-time properties, such as button presses by the driver, only need to be authorized when transmitted, thus reducing the number of streams significantly. Further, Figure 4.12 depicts the maximum setup latency of all streams in the vehicle. By contrast, Figure 4.13 shows the individual setup latencies of all streams in two architecture configurations. It is to be noted that a large number of streams experience lower latencies than the overall system latency given in Figure 4.12. Thus, the stream setup could be prioritized, ensuring that streams required earlier are authorized earlier. The scheduling of stream setups according to priorities is an optimization topic in itself and is out-of-scope of this work.

When analyzing Figure 4.12, the exponential behavior is to be noted. This results from the additionally required authorization messages including the symmetric stream key for additional receivers. The resulting increase is acceptable even for large systems with 500 messages, as shown in Figure 4.12. Increases beyond this number of messages are unlikely in the automotive domain.

The clustering of messages can be explained through the architecture generation. To model a realistic system, where messages are received and processed by multiple components, the number of receivers is increased by 1 every 25 streams. As the additional receiver also needs a grant message with the stream key, the start-up time rises.

When comparing software and hardware supported implementations of LASAN, the advantage of hardware supported implementations can be clearly seen (see Figure 4.12). By utilizing the increasingly existing hardware accelerators in ECUs, in a system with 500 message streams the start-up time can be reduced from 13.18s to 2.97s. Table 4.2 compares the delays introduced by LASAN into a single stream setup. If ECU authentication is completed and hardware support is available, a stream can be set up in less than 2ms. This is by far sufficient when comparing it with most conventional messages, such as in the electric test vehicle EVA (see Chapter 2). EVA is a fully functional electric taxi, built as a research platform by TUM CREATE, supporting research into electric vehicles. In EVA, no message is transmitted with a period under 20ms and all messages are specified to tolerate a delay of up to 80ms. Modern ADASs might have more strict requirements below 10ms, but even here, the setup time is still appropriate. Additionally, for extremely high real-time constraints, a stream can be authorized at vehicle startup, reducing the setup delay required at the time of message transmission to zero.

Future Architectures. Future automotive architectures are expected to supply more bandwidth, computational power and memory, while at the same time reducing the overall number of ECUs. This ECU consolidation will lead to LASAN gaining efficiency in the future. The higher computational power and memory can support larger key lengths and stronger cryptographic measures while driving down the latencies LASAN is currently experiencing. The higher bandwidth will further contribute to a reduction in stream setup latencies. ECU consolidation, also with the possible consolidation of message streams, would decrease vehicle

ECU Authentication	Setup Latency	
	Hardware	Software
included	1.4s	2.3s
not included	0.0016s	0.0046s

Table 4.2: *Stream setup latencies using LASAN for a single stream in ideal conditions (2 ECUs, single bus, no cross traffic).*

start-up delays in LASAN, as delays are mostly dependent on the number of receivers and message streams.

Summary. As shown in the preceding evaluations, LASAN offers low latency stream authorization, while keeping ECU authentication in acceptable boundaries. Compared to existing authentication frameworks LASAN performs highly efficiently, lowering latencies in typical network sizes of 60 to 100 ECUs by on average factor 49 for TESLA and factor 234 for TLS. Yet, LASAN can be improved by scheduling stream authorization based on priority and only when required. This way, stream authorization overhead can be reduced down to 1.6ms, a value acceptable for all but the applications with the strictest real-time requirements. For these applications, streams can be set up a priori, before real-time responses are required.

4.8   Concluding Remarks and Future Work

In this Chapter we present the design, evaluation, verification and integration of the Lightweight Authentication for Secure Automotive Networks (LASAN) and the In-Vehicle Network Simulator (IVNS). We designed LASAN to achieve high performance, even in environments with low computational power and network bandwidth. We showed that the protocols contained in LASAN can be verified with standard network protocol verification tools and thus are proven to be secure to known attacks. We evaluated the performance of LASAN with the IVNS and showed latency decreases of factor 49 to 234 for typical network sizes over existing frameworks, while keeping the security steady. This has been achieved through reducing message sizes, reducing the number of messages, and optimizing use of protocol components for automotive environments. An acceptable loss of runtime flexibility in static automotive networks is compensated for by a secure and real-time capable authentication and authorization of all network participants and messages. As with any digital security measure, the security strength of LASAN is highly dependent on the key length used. With rising computational power and memory, LASAN can make use of greater key lengths, thereby maintaining security. LASAN has further been shown to integrate well with and support existing scenarios in the automotive domain, allowing and supporting secure firmware and ECU replacements and updates from the production of the vehicle till the end-of-life. To the best of our knowledge this is a first for an automotive authentication mechanism.

This Chapter also presents the IVNS, an open source framework for modeling and simulating secure automotive networks, allowing real-time performance analysis. The model includes components and interconnections in automotive networks, a basic configuration, as well as a set of parameters. Parameters can be supplied to tune the components to real-world behavior. IVNS is implemented in Python and is highly modular, allowing easy extensibility. It is available as open source for free use by the research community and industry. By modeling a sufficiently high abstraction level of events, we achieve high performance in terms of computation time and memory requirements, analyzing networks of up to 100 nodes in under 10 minutes, while keeping memory utilization below 300 MBytes. The usefulness of the IVNS has been presented in a case study to quantify the real-time behavior of a secure distributed battery management system. By adjusting the architecture slightly, the performance of the system could be increased by close to an order of magnitude.

While this work focused on the evaluation of LASAN, future work will be concerned with optimizing the framework based on the results acquired in this evaluation. By scheduling ECU authentication and stream authorization messages in a priority-based fashion, the performance for individual messages and thus components and control systems can be increased significantly. This can be achieved in the same fashion as optimization for safety-critical applications, while accounting for the security specifics. Further, the security of LASAN, as for every security measure, heavily depends on the correctness of the implementation. To guarantee this, a reference implementation of LASAN and the discrete event simulation used for evaluation is planned to be published as open source. Further, the basic verification of LASAN, as shown in this work, shall be extended to allow verification of real-world LASAN implementations (Hardware-in-the-Loop).

5

Flexible and Reliable
Message Scheduling in FlexRay

5.1 Problem Description and Summary

The amount of software and Electronic Control Units (ECUs) in cars is continuously increasing. New Advanced Driver Assistance Systems (ADASs) are one of the major selling points of vehicles and rely heavily on the use of software to achieve the required functionality. These applications are not implemented on one single ECU, but distributed over multiple ECUs. To achieve the desired functionality, communication between the ECUs is required. Furthermore, to secure these vehicle networks, the transmission of large and infrequent messages, e.g., for authorization, may be required. When defining a communication system, either an event-triggered or a time-triggered architecture needs to be selected.

In time-triggered, or Time Division Multiple Access (TDMA), systems, each message is assigned a time slot in which it is transmitted. The assignment of messages to time slots is called a schedule. This schedule is usually repeated infinitely. TDMA allows easy calculation of the Worst Case Response Times (WCRTs), as the schedule is fixed at time of implementation and usually not changed at runtime. These WCRTs rely on the assignment of messages to time slots. A message always has to wait until the assigned time slot repeats, before it can be sent. This can lead to high WCRTs, if a message misses its slot. TDMA schedules do not allow preemption. A TDMA system might lead to oversampling, when a message cycle time is not equal to, or a multiple of, the schedule duration. Additionally, as the sizes of time slots are fixed, it is usually not possible to transmit messages longer than one slot length.

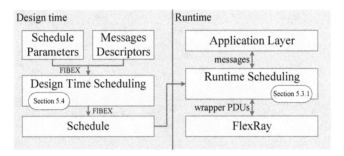

Figure 5.1: *Framework for policy-based scheduling in time-triggered networks. A design time scheduling approach determines a slot to ECU assignment for a set of messages. During runtime our scheduler then assigns the event-triggered messages created in the application layer to communication slots depending on their priority.*

By contrast, event-triggered systems transmit messages as required, allowing more flexibility in message transmissions and a higher utilization of the underlying bus system. An arbitration process is used to avoid collisions of messages transmitted on the bus. Due to the option to transmit messages at any point in time and the arbitration process of an event-triggered system, it can be difficult to calculate the WCRTs. For example, the generally accepted WCRT calculations for the widely applied Controller Area Network (CAN) bus have been shown to be incomplete only after 13 years [168, 20].

When using large and infrequent messages, such as typically used in authentication mechanisms (see Chapter 4), time-triggered systems require a large amount of bandwidth to be reserved statically at design time. At runtime, however, such reservations might only be used very infrequently. Furthermore, in most time-triggered systems, authentication messages will exceed the length of an individual timeslot and no provisions for segmentation of messages exist. These aspects make time-triggered systems, which are a necessity for real-time behavior, inefficient or even impossible to be used in secure communication environments. The efficient transmission of messages with the above characteristics is essential to enable security on time-triggered systems.

This chapter proposes a virtual communication layer which enables policy-based scheduling in time-triggered networks. Figure 5.1 presents our framework, consisting of a design time scheduling determining a slot to ECU assignment, and a priority-based runtime scheduler, supporting message preemption. It enables incremental changes and significantly decreases the complexity of time-triggered systems. Furthermore, it allows to transmit large messages, longer than the length of one time slot and allows more efficient reservation for infrequent messages, thus supporting security mechanisms, such as authentication frameworks. As the introduced virtual communication layer complies with the underlying time-triggered transmission scheme,

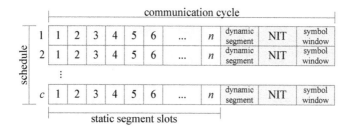

Figure 5.2: *FlexRay schedule with n slots in the static segment, dynamic segment, Network Idle Time (NIT), symbol window and repetitive schedule containing c communication cycles.*

it enables mixed criticality systems supporting concurrent time- and event-triggered communication. This enables the introduction of security mechanisms, such as authentication protocols into legacy time-triggered communication mechanisms.

FlexRay. The proposed framework is implemented for the time-triggered segment of the FlexRay bus. FlexRay is an automotive communication system with a bandwidth of up to 10 Mbit/s, incorporating TDMA and an event-triggered segment into one schedule. In FlexRay, TDMA is called the static segment and the event-triggered segment is called the dynamic segment. A FlexRay schedule is organized into a fixed number of cycles c. Each cycle is divided into static and dynamic segment, as well as synchronization segments (see Figure 5.2). Over the runtime of a FlexRay system, the schedule is repeated infinitely.

Each cycle of the static segment is further subdivided into time slots. The time-triggered communication in the static segment allows for a straight-forward calculation of response times. The priority-based arbitration in the dynamic segment, however, makes it difficult to calculate response times [149]. By contrast, policy-based scheduling ensures strict priorities per ECU and easy to compute WCRTs.

Contributions. To allow the implementation of security mechanisms with infrequent large messages on existing time-triggered communication systems, this work proposes (1) an architecture for policy-based scheduling of event-triggered messages in time-triggered communication systems, (2) a set of scheduling algorithms to schedule policy-based messages to time-triggered slots, and (3) a prototypical implementation of this scheduling approach for FlexRay.

Policy-based scheduling is achieved by adding a virtual event-triggered layer on top of a time-triggered communication system. This virtual communication layer allows a higher flexibility in message sizes and lower latencies than the underlying time-triggered system through message preemption. The increased flexibility for both, timeslots and message lengths, can be used in conjunction with authentication frameworks, allowing the transmission of large, infrequent messages highly efficiently. Application layer messages can be scheduled event-triggered, based on predefined policies such as priority-based scheduling, and guarantees for message deliveries can be given. Worst-case response times can be calculated for all messages and the schedulability of the system can be easily verified.

The proposed approach is fully compatible with time-triggered communication systems and can be used side-by-side on the same physical bus, without interference. Changes to and addition of new messages to the communication system are simple, as recomputation of the time-triggered schedule can be avoided.

Policy-based scheduling has been implemented for the time-triggered FlexRay static segment. This is achieved by assigning slots to ECUs, instead of messages. Messages are then scheduled per ECU at run-time, based on priority and arrival time. To integrate the policy-based scheduling with existing FlexRay toolchains, standardized FIBEX input and output is employed. Finally, the developed framework has been evaluated regarding bandwidth utilization and WCRTs.

Organization of this chapter. This chapter is organized as follows. Section 5.2 gives an overview over the existing literature on the combination of time- and event-triggered systems, as well as scheduling for the FlexRay static and dynamic segment. Furthermore, the differences of policy-based scheduling to all existing approaches are discussed. Section 5.3 introduces the architecture of policy-based scheduling and discusses possible runtime scheduling algorithms. In Section 5.4, a heuristic algorithm and an Integer Linear Program (ILP) approach to policy-based scheduling for FlexRay are proposed. Section 5.5 presents several tests to evaluate the performance of policy-based scheduling on FlexRay, in comparison to conventional scheduling algorithms. Section 5.6 summarizes the proposed approach and concludes.

5.2   Related Work

In the following, an overview of existing time-triggered architectures and their approaches to scheduling, is given. Additionally, timing analysis and scheduling algorithms for the static and dynamic segment of conventional FlexRay are discussed. Other approaches for event-triggered scheduling in TDMA systems are illustrated and differences to the proposed approach are clarified.

Time-triggered architectures. A basic time-triggered architecture is presented in [84]. Based on this time-triggered architecture, scheduling algorithms have been developed, allowing reliable and predictable transmission of data. Some of these approaches consider the message transmission itself [41, 172], while others follow a holistic approach and view the message transmissions in context with the message generating tasks [99]. All of these approaches employ fixed timeslots, as described in [84], and are thus limited in message lengths and asynchronous scheduling capabilities.

FlexRay static segment. The analysis of time-triggered systems concerning response times and scheduling has also been conducted for the time-triggered static segment of FlexRay. Multiple approaches have been proposed to schedule messages in the conventional FlexRay static segment. Based on the AUTOSAR standard, [38] proposes a heuristic approach for scheduling messages, maximizing the bandwidth utilization. This assumes, however, that all message lengths equal the slot length and only one message is sent in every frame. The problem of message fragmentation is addressed in [96]. There, a heuristic and an ILP are used to optimize the bandwidth utilization in the form of a bin packing problem.

The optimization of message jitter and the number of frames used in the system is the primary target in [150] and [151]. As a measurement for the efficiency of the approach, jitter and bandwidth utilization are employed. For optimization of bandwidth, a Non-linear Integer Program (NIP) is employed, while the jitter is optimized with an ILP.

A combination of task and message scheduling is addressed in [181]. As a measure for efficiency, the control performance of an example system is used, incorporating latencies and jitters.

FlexRay dynamic segment. In addition to the analysis of the FlexRay static segment, scheduling in the dynamic segment has been researched. The calculation of the WCRT for the FlexRay dynamic segment, as proposed in [182], is highly complex. A scheduling approach for the FlexRay dynamic segment is proposed in [149]. There, the required number of frame IDs and the message jitter are to be minimized. An additional analysis of the FlexRay dynamic segment has been presented in [118]. It considers cycle multiplexing as a method to further reduce the number of required frame IDs. In contrast to the approaches above, this chapter focuses on the static segment and uses preemption for lower response times, as well as introduces possibilities for multi-mode messages.

Event-based messages over TDMA. In [98], an event-triggered layer that is virtually placed on top of the time-triggered architecture from [84] is described. The approach divides every time slot into two segments for time- and event-triggered messages. This achieves a slightly higher flexibility than a conventional time-triggered system, but assumes fixed message lengths. The approach proposed in [16] adds arbitration points to every slot of the time-triggered protocol in [83]. Based on these approaches, response time evaluations have been proposed in [124]. There, a set of parameters is proposed, allowing a good estimation of the worst- and best-case response times for an event-triggered communication layer in a time-triggered system.

An approach to integrate event-triggered communication with the FlexRay static segment is shown in [88]. However, this approach assumes one message per frame and a message length equal to the frame size. Additionally, it is assumed that the message deadline is always equal to the interarrival time of the message. Interarrival times smaller than the length of the schedule are not considered. This dependency leads to an inversion in design. The static segment needs to be modeled after the requirements of the event-triggered layer, as both layers are not independent. In case the parameters of the event-triggered layer are changed, the time-triggered layer needs to be regenerated, or guarantees might be lost.

Hierarchical Scheduling. With the rising complexity of real-time systems, compositional design becomes increasingly important. By dividing a system into subsystems and arranging these in a scheduling hierarchy, the scheduling of such complex systems can be simplified. An approach for hierarchical scheduling has been proposed in [27] and a comparison of different hierarchical scheduling techniques is presented in [2]. In comparison to hierarchical scheduling, policy-based scheduling does not require a scheduling hierarchy. The given communication system is scheduled in the traditional, flat scheduling manner. In policy-based scheduling, the time-triggered schedule is generated at design time, but filled with event-triggered messages at runtime.

Security Integration. To integrate authentication into existing time-triggered systems, other approaches could be used. By utilizing the existing fields in the header or footer of the time-triggered slot, the required bandwidth needed for authentication could be reduced. An approach to this has been presented in [180]. There, a truncated Cipher-based Message Authentication Code (CMAC) is integrated with the Cyclic Redundancy Check (CRC) of the underlying communication system. This ensures integrity of the message, but it can not easily be integrated with the encryption of the message to ensure confidentiality. Furthermore, it does require adaptation of the communication system to allow for the change of the CRC.

This work. This chapter presents an approach to flexibly schedule messages in a virtual event-triggered layer on top of a time-triggered communication infrastructure. The virtual event-triggered layer allows to transmit messages flexibly, while the underlying time-triggered communication system allows us to guarantee message deadlines. In contrast to the work above, this approach supports messages of any length, as well as multiple messages per slot. This enables the implementation of security mechanisms requiring large and infrequent messages, such as authentication frameworks (see Chapter 4). Furthermore, interarrival times of messages can be chosen freely and multiple messages can be sent per schedule repetition. Oversampling of messages is reduced and preemption can be utilized for faster response times. The proposed approach offers flexibility, as messages can be changed easily, without the need for reconfiguration of the complete system. The FlexRay static segment has been used to implement the approach and to verify its feasibility. Additionally, the system proposed in this chapter can be used in parallel with a conventional FlexRay system, sharing the same physical bus, without interference or the need for adaptation of the existing specification.

5.3   Architecture

This section outlines how time- and event-triggered systems are integrated in policy-based scheduling. While policy-based scheduling is applicable to time-triggered systems in general, we use FlexRay terminology to describe our system. No definitions and parameters from the FlexRay standard have been altered, thus achieving full compatibility to conventional FlexRay systems. Instead, we reserve time slots in the static segment and assign these to ECUs. We call the messages used to reserve a time slot in the static segment wrapper Protocol Data Units (PDUs). In the proposed approach, a wrapper PDU always fills the static slot in its entirety. These wrapper PDUs are coordinated by the communication layer introduced for policy-based scheduling. This additional layer is logically placed between the application layer and the conventional FlexRay communication layer of every ECU (see Figure 5.1).

At runtime, messages from the application layer can arrive at any point in time, i.e. event-triggered, and the policy-based communication layer is sorting these messages into wrapper PDUs and thus FlexRay static slots. This way, a virtual event-triggered layer is created on top of the time-triggered FlexRay static segment. To reserve sufficient time slots for all messages to be transmitted, the time-triggered schedule needs to be calculated, based on the message parameters of the application layer. This calculation is described in Section 5.4. With this calculation and the correct mapping of event-triggered messages to time slots, it can be ensured that every deadline in the system is satisfied.

5.3.1   Runtime Scheduling Algorithm

In the following, the scheduling of messages into timeslots at runtime is explained. The additional communication layer is required to add application layer messages to slots of the static segment. This is performed according to a fixed algorithm on the ECU at runtime. Many suitable scheduling algorithms are available in literature, such as First Come First Serve (FCFS), Round Robin (RR), Shortest Message First (SMF), Priority-based, Multi-Level Queues and Multi-Level Feedback Queues. Based on the requirements existing in vehicles, a suitable scheduling algorithm needs to be found.

In vehicles, some messages always have a higher priority than others. Consider an Anti-lock Braking System (ABS) system versus a park distance sensor. Even when parking, the vehicle brakes need to be able to react reliably. This makes schemes like FCFS, RR and SMF unsuitable. These schemes would not represent the priorities in vehicles accurately. As multi-level feedback queues are also changing this priority behavior, they do not fulfill the requirements for vehicles. A multi-level queue could be used if the individual queues are served in a strict priority-based fashion. This, however, equals priority-based scheduling. Thus, the scheduling of event-triggered messages to timeslots is chosen to be strictly priority-based with FCFS, if two messages of the same priority are queued. The priorities for messages can be determined in any fashion, as required by the user.

For the application shown in the following, priorities are generated based on Earliest Deadline First (EDF) scheduling, with longer messages having higher priority, if two deadlines are equal. The strict adherence to priorities in the policy-based scheduling allows for mixed criticality applications to be implemented and to guarantee the delivery of all messages within their required deadline.

5.3.2 Multi-Mode Applications

The proposed framework is designed such that different priorities per message can be considered at various times. This allows to integrate multi-mode applications for different situations the vehicle experiences very efficiently. For example, authentication messages can be assigned higher priority when the vehicle is not in use, to facilitate faster authentication. At startup, message authorizations take precedence and once started, highest priority is given to safety-critical real-time messages. The proposed approach allows to define multiple modes for different situations the vehicle experiences. These modes are required to be exclusive and non-overlapping. The algorithm automatically selects the minimum set of messages required to transmit all data without deadline violations. Due to the inherent flexibility of policy-based scheduling, this results in a smaller amount of messages for the overall schedule than in a conventional scheduling approach where oversampling is required.

5.3.3 Wrapper PDUs

When placing application layer messages into wrapper PDUs and, consequently, into time slots, the borders of time slots are factored out. The sum of all wrapper PDUs for one ECU appears as one continuous communication channel to the application layer. This allows the transmission of messages longer than the length of one static slot, e.g. for diagnosis or programming of ECUs, by continuing messages in following timeslots. However, the loss of time slot boundaries also leads to two issues. First, receiving ECUs can not identify separate messages anymore, as there are no time slots or other start/end indicators for messages inside a wrapper PDU (Segmentation). Second, the implicit addressing scheme which is inherent to TDMA slots is lost (Addressing). Receiving ECUs have no possibility to identify which type of message is transmitted or to which ECU a message is addressed. To solve these two issues, an additional header is introduced to be transmitted with every application layer message. As this header introduces overhead into the system, it needs to be as small as possible.

In the following, the issues are addressed and the fields of the message header are introduced:

Segmentation. To distinguish two messages, a length field is introduced into the header. This 8 bits long field allows to specify the length of the following payload up to a maximum of 255 bytes. This header can be placed in multiple positions, such as in the beginning of every wrapper PDU, allowing a higher bandwidth efficiency by combining the headers of all included messages. This placement, however, reduces flexibility, as all messages transmitted in one wrapper PDU need to be known at the start of the wrapper PDU. Messages arriving late could not be added. Placing the header in front of every application layer message (see Figure 5.3) allows a higher flexibility, as high priority messages arriving late can still be added while the slot transmission is in progress.

Addressing. In a time-triggered system, the assignment of messages to time slots also contains an implicit addressing scheme. Due to the placement of application layer messages into the continuous communication channel generated by wrapper PDUs, this implicit addressing information is lost. In TDMA, every transmitting ECU knows where each message is to be transmitted and each receiving ECU knows how to interpret a received message in a timeslot, as only one type of message is allowed for transmission at any one position in the schedule. To compensate for this, a message type field is introduced into the header of every application layer message. This is a 16-bit field, describing the type of the message. The addressing is similar to the approach as it is done in the FlexRay dynamic segment. A message type field of 16-bit allows 65536 different message types. This amount is sufficient for most FlexRay communication. It is the same value as used in the FlexRay dynamic segment. With the introduction of this field, the addressing information is restored and the receiving ECUs are able to process the message.

In addition to the header in front of every application layer message, a header of 8 bits length, called preemption indicator (PI), is added to every wrapper PDU. This header allows to implement preemption in a time-triggered system. In case a high priority message arrives, while a low priority message is transmitting, the high priority message may interrupt the lower priority message at the beginning of the next timeslot. The preemption indicator is used to signal the number of preempting messages at the beginning of a timeslot. The preempting messages are transmitted first, afterwards, the lower priority message is continued as illustrated in Figure 5.3. This work does not consider non-preemptive scheduling. As preemptive scheduling yields significantly lower latencies at the cost of only minimal overheads in the waiting queues of ECUs and slightly less net bandwidth on the bus, the non-preemptive case does not add any advantages.

5.4 Design-Time Scheduling

In the following, a scheduling algorithm is developed which allows the transmission of application layer messages in event-triggered fashion. The scheduling algorithm creates a time-triggered schedule for the policy-based communication layer. This is based on the application layer messages to be scheduled in the policy-based approach.

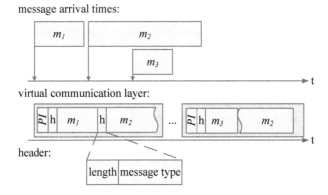

Figure 5.3: *Preemptive scheduling of application layer messages for the proposed approach with continuous virtual communication channel. The arrows mark arrivals of messages. Message m_3 arrives after message m_2, but the priority of m_3 is greater than the priority of m_2. The messages do not need to be placed in consecutive slots.*

For the time-triggered layer, a schedule needs to be generated, incorporating all wrapper PDUs. This scheduling is performed at time of implementation. Two approaches have been developed for this contribution, a heuristic and an ILP. While it is well established to use a heuristic for FlexRay scheduling, the developed ILP shall serve as a benchmark for the heuristic, showing the optimal solution to the given problem. Both approaches are described in the following.

For both approaches, heuristic and ILP, minor differences exist for the different FlexRay versions. While FlexRay 2.1A requires that each slot in every cycle contains the same message type, FlexRay 3.0.1 allows to assign different message types to slots in different cycles (see Figure 5.4). The developed algorithms account for these differences.

In the following, the terms message and application layer message refer to a message descriptor, including length, period and deadline, not a specific message with content to be sent on the bus.

The expected input to the scheduler is a set of application layer messages to be scheduled. Additionally, the parameters of the schedule need to be defined. These include the number of static slots, the slot size, the number of cycles and the cycle length, among others. A reservation for predefined time-triggered messages, which are transmitted within the conventional FlexRay static segment can be added as well. The slots occupied by these messages will not be used to schedule wrapper PDUs, thus achieving coexistence with conventional FlexRay.

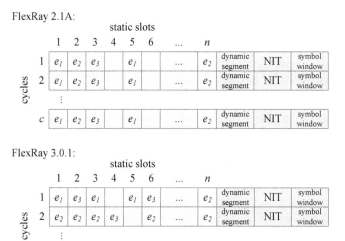

Figure 5.4: *Comparison of FlexRay 2.1A and 3.0.1 scheduling. For FlexRay 2.1A we only consider one cycle to assign an ECU. For FlexRay 3.0.1 the whole schedule is considered, as multiple ECUs can share one slot. The basis of assignment is one frame.*

The deadline of every message is used as a priority indicator, with a shorter deadline equaling a higher priority. This ensures that all deadlines are satisfied, as the message queues are ordered along message deadlines.

The set M of application layer messages m to be scheduled is described by the following tuple:

$$m = (N, s, R, l^m, t_p^m, t_d^m), m \in M \qquad (5.1)$$

with

- N: name of m, a unique string in the FlexRay cluster,
- s: sender, name of the ECU sending m,
- R: receivers, list of receiving ECUs,
- l^m: length of m in bytes,
- t_p^m: period of m in milliseconds,
- t_d^m: deadline of m in milliseconds.

All messages are sent and received by an ECU e, with e being part of the set of all ECUs in the cluster, $e \in E$.

A schedule is defined by the following parameters:

- c: number of cycles, required,
- n: number of static slots per cycle, required,
- t_{dc}: duration of cycle in milliseconds, required,
- t_{ds}: duration of static slot in milliseconds, required,
- b: length of one static slot in bytes, required,
- M_p: set of predefined messages, optional.

Based on these inputs, both scheduling algorithms, heuristic and ILP, described in the following, calculate an assignment of static slots to ECUs. To ensure compatibility to conventional FlexRay, a minimal set of placeholder messages is generated from these assignments that is used to reserve slots in the FlexRay schedule. These place holder messages are the described wrapper PDUs.

5.4.1 Heuristic

This section describes the heuristic approach to policy-based message scheduling. An algorithm has been developed, using the application layer messages and schedule parameters as input to calculate the assignment of static slots to ECUs. The required number of slots per cycle and frames for the complete schedule are determined for FlexRay 2.1A and FlexRay 3.0.1, respectively. The heuristic processes the input data in two steps:

1. slot distance calculation
2. slot allocation

In the first step, the maximum distance between two slots for every application layer message of an ECU is calculated, such that the deadline for every message is met. The second step allocates all slots into the schedule with the given parameters, adjusting message and slot distances, such that all messages fit the schedule.

1) Slot distance calculation.   The first part of the heuristic calculates the required number of slots and frames for the schedule, based on the bandwidth requirements of each ECU. The bandwidth is determined by the periods, sizes and lengths of messages, as well as their deadlines. A value dist_e is calculated for every ECU e, describing the distance two consecutive slots can be allocated apart, such that all bandwidth and deadline requirements are fulfilled.

The upper bound of the WCRT $r_{\mathrm{dist}_e}(m)$ for a message in terms of slot lengths needs to be calculated. This calculation is based on the distance between two slots (see Equation 5.6) for an ECU and the WCRT $r_{\mathrm{hp}}(m)$ of all higher priority messages on this ECU:

$$\forall e \in E, \forall m \in M_e : r_{\text{dist}_e}(m) = \text{dist}_e + (\text{dist}_e \cdot r_{\text{hp}}(m)) \tag{5.2}$$

The utilization of all higher priority messages describes the delay $r_{\text{hp}}(m)$ caused to a message and is based on the deadline t_d^m of message m, as well as the period $t_p^{\tilde{m}}$ and the length $l^{\tilde{m}}$ of all higher priority messages $\tilde{m}$ of message m. This delay is normalized to the slot length b:

$$r_{\text{hp}}(m) = \frac{1}{b} \cdot \left(\sum_{\tilde{m} \in \text{hp}(m)} \left(\frac{t_d^m}{t_p^{\tilde{m}}} \cdot l^{\tilde{m}} \right) \right) \tag{5.3}$$

The response time $r_{\text{dist}_e}(m)$ for every message m needs to be shorter than the deadline t_d^m and the distance dist_e between two slots needs to be lower than the maximum distance between two slots for one ECU:

$$r_{\text{dist}_e}(m) \le t_d^m \tag{5.4}$$

$$\text{dist}_e \le \text{dist}_{e,\text{max}} \tag{5.5}$$

The maximum distance is computed from the available number of slots n in a cycle and the required number of slots $s_{c,e}$ for an ECU e.

$$\text{dist}_{e,\text{max}} = \frac{n}{s_{c,e}} \tag{5.6}$$

The required number of slots $s_{c,e}$ is determined by the overall number of slots $slots_e$ for one ECU, divided by the number of cycles c. As only complete slots can be allocated, this number needs to be an integer value. To ensure a sufficient number of slots in the cycle, this value is rounded to the next higher integer number:

$$s_{c,e} = \left\lceil \frac{slots_e}{c} \right\rceil \tag{5.7}$$

The required number of slots per ECU $slots_e$ is based on the duration of the schedule $t_{dc} \cdot c$, the periods t_p^m of all messages $m \in M_e$ and the lengths l^m of these messages:

$$slots_e = \frac{1}{b} \cdot \sum_{m \in M_e} \frac{t_{dc} \cdot c}{t_p^m} \cdot l^m \tag{5.8}$$

This describes the bandwidth requirement of the ECU. The bandwidth is normalized to one slot length b.

Based on these equations, the maximum distance between two consecutive slots of one ECU is defined by the maximum distance that satisfies the deadline requirement of all messages $m \in M_e$ for this ECU:

$$\arg\max_{\text{dist}_e \in \mathbb{N}} \{ r_{\text{dist}_e}(m) \le t_d^m \ \forall m \in M_e \} \tag{5.9}$$

2) Slot allocation.   After the distances between messages have been determined for each ECU, the allocation of slots is described in the following, as depicted in Figure 5.5 for FlexRay 2.1A. These steps are executed for all ECUs in ascending order of their previously calculated slot distance $dist_e$. The slot allocation starts with the first free slot in the cycle (see Figure 5.5 (1)). Based on this slot, all other slots are allocated in distance $dist_e$ apart (2). This placement also adjusts for the dynamic segment, Network Idle Time (NIT) and symbol window. The slot allocation completes when sufficient slots are placed throughout the complete schedule in distance $dist_e$ (3). This also considers the distance between the last slot and the first slot of every schedule to adjust for the final dynamic segment, NIT and symbol window. Should any of these steps fail for any ECU, because the shortest available slot distance is too long, a deadline violation may occur and the system is considered not schedulable (4). In case all steps succeed, the algorithm terminates with the correctly allocated results (5).

The slot allocation for FlexRay 3.0.1 is performed similarly to the calculations for FlexRay 2.1A. In contrast to FlexRay 2.1A, FlexRay 3.0.1 supports the assignment of identical slots in different cycles to different ECUs (see Figure 5.4). This allows more flexibility in allocating the slots. To accommodate this flexibility, the algorithm has been adjusted to calculate the slots over one complete schedule ($c \cdot n$ slots), instead of one cycle (n slots). This results in a few additional checks to cover the dynamic segment, NIT and symbol window at the end of every cycle. As FlexRay 3.0.1 does not require the assignment of a slot in every cycle, $dist_e$ might be longer than the shortest deadline for an ECU. To accommodate this, the algorithm continuously checks the deadline constraint when allocating slots. Additionally, the end condition (see Figure 5.5 (3)) has been adjusted to incorporate a full schedule instead of one cycle.

5.4.2   Integer Linear Program (ILP)

In the following, an ILP formulation which determines an optimal slot to sender, or frame to sender, assignment for FlexRay 2.1A or 3.0.1, respectively, is presented. While an ILP allows to find the optimal solution to a given problem, it does not scale well. Thus, the proposed ILP shall be used as a benchmark, evaluating the performance of the heuristic, wherever possible.

The ILP determines a schedule with minimal bandwidth utilization. The ILP approach is based on the following constants and variables:

- $n_{all} = \left\lceil \frac{t_{dc}}{t_{ds}} \right\rceil$: theoretical number of slots fitting in one cycle including the dynamic segment.

- P_e: set containing all message periods t_p^m for an ECU e.

- $x_{k,e}$: binary variable indicating if slot/frame k is occupied by ECU e (1) or not (0).

To support both FlexRay 2.1A and 3.0.1, the constant n_{tot} is introduced, defining the number of frames the ILP considers. For FlexRay 2.1A n_{tot} equals the number of slots for one cycle, as slots might not be shared between senders:

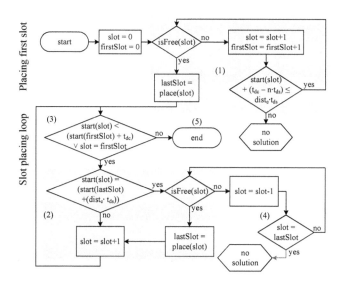

Figure 5.5: *FlexRay 2.1A scheduling algorithm for slot allocation. Based on the initial slot found in the first part of the algorithm, other slots are allocated a maximum of* dist$_e$ *slots apart. The function isFree(x) determines if slot x is in use by another ECU and the function start(x) returns the start time of slot x. These calculations are performed for every ECU.*

$$n_{\text{tot}} = n_{\text{all}} \tag{5.10}$$

For FlexRay 3.0.1 n_{tot} equals the number of frames for all cycles allowing to divide the slot among multiple ECUs:

$$n_{\text{tot}} = c \cdot n_{\text{all}} \tag{5.11}$$

The objective of the ILP formulation is to minimize the number of occupied frames:

$$\min \sum_{\forall e \in E} \sum_{k \in \{0,1,..,n_{\text{tot}}-1\}} \mathbf{x}_{k,e} \tag{5.12}$$

For a certain message period t_p^m, a minimal number of slots has to be assigned to fulfill the bandwidth and deadline requirements of all messages m with periods of t_p^m. This is considered for every message m of every ECU e in Equation 5.13. The number of slots required is determined by the length of the message l^m, normalized to one slot length b. The right-hand side also considers preemption of messages m by higher priority messages $\tilde{m}$ with a deadline $t_p^{\tilde{m}}$ shorter than the message deadline t_p^m. The deadline requirement is ensured on the left-hand side by placing at least one slot within every period t_p^m. To ensure that the first and the last frame also keep the maximal distance, the modulo operation % ensures that also the first element in the schedule is considered:

$$\forall e \in E, i \in \{0, 1, .., n_{\text{tot}} - 1\}, t_p^m \in P_e:$$

$$\sum_{k \in \{i,...,i+\left\lfloor \frac{t_p^m}{t_{ds}} \right\rfloor -1\}} \mathbf{x}_{k\%n_{\text{tot}},e} \geq \tag{5.13}$$

$$\left\lceil \sum_{\tilde{m} \in \{\tilde{m}|t_p^{\tilde{m}} \leq t_p^m, \tilde{m} \in M_e\}} \frac{t_p^m}{t_p^{\tilde{m}}} \cdot \frac{l^m}{b} \right\rceil$$

For all ECUs, no frames shall be placed outside the static segment:

$$\forall e \in E, k \in \{0, 1, .., n_{\text{tot}} - 1\}, \exists k\%n_{\text{all}} > n:$$

$$\mathbf{x}_{k,e} = 0 \tag{5.14}$$

For every frame in the schedule, it needs to be ensured that two ECUs cannot occupy the same frame:

$$k \in \{0, 1, .., n_{\text{tot}} - 1\}, \exists k\%n_{\text{all}} < n:$$

$$\sum_{\forall e \in E} \mathbf{x}_{k,e} = 1 \tag{5.15}$$

The solution of the ILP delivers the assignment of slots and frames to ECUs for FlexRay 2.1A and FlexRay 3.0.1, respectively. This is used to reserve timeslots in the FlexRay static segment, in the form of wrapper PDUs.

5.5   Experimental Results

In this section, the policy-based scheduling is evaluated and compared against the conventional approach from [96]. For this purpose, a FlexRay scheduling framework, including the policy-based heuristic and ILP scheduling, has been implemented in Java, allowing to compare the scheduling algorithms to the framework from [96]. The developed scheduling framework is connected to the development toolchain via Field Bus Exchange Format (FIBEX). FIBEX is a standardized data format for the exchange of data related to bus systems between tools. It is based on Extensible Markup Language (XML) and is the standard data exchange format for

FlexRay systems. The proposed system supports import and export for FIBEX versions 2.0.1 and 3.1.

To evaluate the performance of the developed algorithms for FlexRay, the input parameters are varied and the output is surveyed. The performance is measured in terms of bandwidth and WCRT. Additionally, the computational performance of the different approaches is evaluated. The input to all algorithms consists of externally generated and verified FlexRay parameters, as well as a set of messages to be scheduled. To accommodate for statistical variations in the message sets, multiple sets have been generated for every test. The FlexRay system is defined by a cycle duration t_{dc} of 5ms, 62 static slots per cycle (n), a slot size b of 42 bytes and 64 cycles per schedule (c). The set of messages is generated randomly from a set of given parameters. The parameters are varied for the different testcases and described below.

The metrics for comparison are the average number of slots and frames of the scheduling runs, for FlexRay 2.1A and FlexRay 3.0.1, respectively. As the number of slots and frames represent the bus utilization, a lower number of slots and frames is better. In addition to the average number of slots and frames, error margins are given in the form of the standard deviation from the average value over the set of generated schedules.

It is important to note that the conventional scheduling approach assumes an AUTOSAR architecture, requiring one byte at the beginning of every slot for administrative information and is thus working on a slot length of $b = 41$ bytes. Similarly, the policy-based approach requires one byte as preemption indicator and thus also works with $b = 41$ bytes available for payload.

For all testcases, multi-mode messages have been employed. The messages have been generated such that 50% of all messages in a testcase have two modes. For all multi-mode messages, the period and size of a message may vary for the modes. However, it is guaranteed that a longer or equal period always contains a longer or equal message size.

5.5.1 Size Variations

To determine the performance of policy-based message scheduling under different message lengths, the average size of all messages in the system is varied. This is achieved by adjusting the distribution of message sizes, starting from the distribution used in [96]. The test is repeated multiple times, as the set of messages is generated in a statistical process. The results for this test are shown in Figure 5.6. The size distributions of all messages in the system are varied and sorted by increasing average message size. The last two sets of messages include messages with length longer than one slot. These messages are important to facilitate security in the communication system. As shown in Chapter 4, authentication messages are very long, exceeding the slot lengths specified for most time-triggered systems. By utilizing the virtual communication layer, such messages can be scheduled on FlexRay, allowing the implementation of authentication frameworks over time-triggered systems, such as FlexRay. The message length used here is 64 bytes, the minimum length of an Ethernet frame.

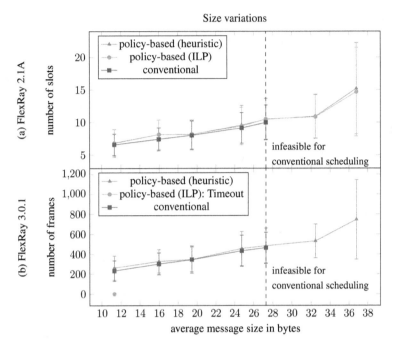

Figure 5.6: *Number of slots and frames required for scheduling with FlexRay 2.1A and FlexRay 3.0.1 for different average message sizes. The system contains 100 different messages and 5 ECUs.*

As it can be seen from Figure 5.6, the conventional scheduling fails to process messages longer than one slot length, thus failing to schedule the given sets of messages. All shown testcases with size variations are based on 58 different periods. Policy-based scheduling can schedule any message length, independent from the slot length in the static segment.

FlexRay 2.1A.   As can be seen in Figure 5.6(a), for smaller message sizes, the policy-based scheduling performance about matches the performance of conventional scheduling. For larger message sizes of more than one slot length, the conventional scheduling fails to perform its task, while the policy-based approach can continue to schedule messages. The minimum difference between the two approaches is 2%, while the maximum difference is 8.7%. However, for larger message sizes, a comparison is not possible, as the conventional algorithm fails to schedule these messages. This is due to the fact that in a conventional FlexRay scheduling algorithm, the maximum allowed message size is equal to the slot length. By contrast, the policy-based message scheduling can schedule messages of arbitrary lengths. While the FlexRay system is not fully utilized, the policy-based scheduling will always be able to accommodate messages, even if the longest message length is larger than one slot length.

FlexRay 3.0.1.   Figure 5.6(b) shows the scheduling results for FlexRay 3.0.1. For smaller message sizes, the policy-based scheduling performance almost matches the conventional scheduling. For larger message sizes of more than one slot length, the conventional scheduling fails to find a solution, while the policy-based approach can continue to schedule messages.

Due to the structure of FlexRay 3.0.1, being able to assign frames instead of slots, the complexity of the problem size increases significantly. The increase in complexity of the problem leads to an exponential growth of the constraints and variables in the ILP. Thus, the comparison for FlexRay 3.0.1 is based on the heuristic approach for conventional and policy-based FlexRay, as the ILPs for both approaches can not be calculated with reasonable resources (see Section 5.5.4). For small messages, the performance difference between the two approaches varies between 0.4% and 13%. Additionally, like in FlexRay 2.1A, the conventional approach is not capable of scheduling messages larger than one slot size, leaving the larger message sets as not schedulable. Again, the policy-based approach can utilize its continuous communication channel to also schedule messages with length longer than one slot and thus is able to schedule all given message sets.

5.5.2   Latency

Besides the higher flexibility in message lengths, the policy-based scheduling also allows lower WCRTs for all messages in the system than a purely time-triggered system. To verify policy-based scheduling with regard to deadlines and to calculate WCRTs, we employ Real-Time Calculus (RTC) [165]. RTC is an extension of network calculus, tailored to real-time systems [92]. Similar to network calculus, real-time calculus allows to compute the arrival and service curves for a communication system. Based on the Modular Performance Analysis [176], implemented in the RTC Toolbox, the proposed approach is analyzed, to verify that the deadlines of all messages are met. The service and arrival curves are generated from the slot and frame assignment determined per ECU by the proposed algorithm and the set of messages supplied by the user, respectively. Based on the slot and frame assignment from the proposed algorithm, RTC calculates the WCRTs for all messages on all ECUs. These WCRTs are compared to the message deadlines. This way, it can be ensured that all messages meet their deadlines at any point in time.

Additionally, the WCRTs are compared to those of a conventional FlexRay system. The results for FlexRay 2.1A and FlexRay 3.0.1 are shown in Figure 5.7. In conventional FlexRay scheduling, a message can only be transmitted at a fixed place in the TDMA scheme. Thus, the WCRT of any message is equal to its period, or the oversampling required by the scheduling algorithm. As we are using a set of periods which does not require oversampling, the WCRTs for conventional FlexRay are equal to the message periods, which in turn, are equal to the message

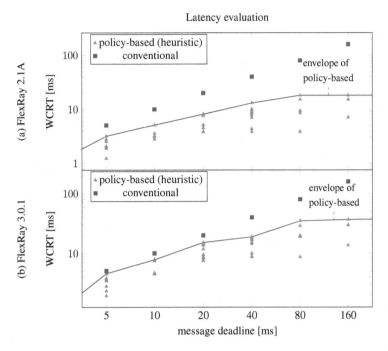

Figure 5.7: *Exemplary worst-case response time (WCRT) analysis for FlexRay 2.1A and FlexRay 3.0.1 for heuristic scheduling of policy-based approach and conventional scheduling. The policy-based scheduling shows a significant improvement in latencies for both FlexRay versions and all messages in the system.*

deadlines, for both heuristic and ILP. From Figure 5.7(a), it can be seen that in policy-based scheduling, the latencies for all messages are significantly shorter than the deadlines achievable in the conventional scheduling approach. This holds for all messages on all ECUs, regardless of their size or deadline. This is due to the flexible EDF scheduling and the implemented preemption capabilities. As messages are not bound to timeslots, far lower worst-case latencies can be achieved. Messages with short deadlines always have a higher priority and can be transmitted first, while messages with longer deadlines are queued. As slots can be allocated more flexibly in FlexRay 3.0.1, compared to FlexRay 2.1A, the differences in latency between policy-based scheduling and conventional scheduling are smaller (see Figure 5.7(b)). However, in absolute terms, improvements of policy-based scheduling over conventional FlexRay are still significant, especially for longer message deadlines. Figure 5.7 omits the ILP approach to policy-based scheduling. The results are in the same range as the results for the heuristic approach.

5.5.3 Period Variations

The second relevant parameter of the message distributions is the set of periods used for the message generation. A higher set of periods allows more flexibility, as the application developer does not require to adjust his application to the communication system, but can freely schedule the application, as required. This can make control algorithms and networks more efficient, as less oversampling and messages are required to reach stable operation. Furthermore, it allows the efficient implementation of infrequent messages, such as used in security frameworks. Authentication and authorization messages are transmitted with a very low frequency, with message periods in the range of days to months. Without policy-based scheduling, these messages would require extreme oversampling, leading to low efficiency of the bus system. The size distribution used for this testcase is taken from [96]. The number of periods has been increased for different message sets, to verify the influence of this parameter on the performance of policy-based scheduling, compared to conventional scheduling.

Conventional FlexRay is optimized for a set of periods defined in the FlexRay standard. This set has been used as a starting point and further periods have been added for other sets. For a cycle time t_{dc} of 5ms, the basic set of periods is defined as 5ms, 10ms, 20ms, 40ms, 80ms, 160ms, 320ms. All periods are integer multiples of one cycle length, as the conventional scheduling algorithm, in contrast to the policy-based scheduling, is not capable of scheduling fraction periods. The results for this test are shown in Figure 5.8 and discussed in the following.

FlexRay 2.1A. When comparing the policy-based approach to the conventional FlexRay scheduling, the performance for a low number of periods is expectedly lower, as the conventional algorithm is optimized for this application (see Figure 5.8(a)). However, when crossing a threshold of 30 different periods in the system, the policy-based approach performs only slightly worse than the conventional algorithm. Although having a smaller net bandwidth, due to overhead in the message headers, performance is nearly equal for a high amount of different periods. It is to note that this testcase is limited to integer periods, as fraction periods cannot be processed by the conventional scheduling algorithm and thus have no basis for comparison. This limits the policy-based approach in its performance. As it is common in combined time- and event-triggered systems, the policy-based approach is a trade-off between the bus utilization on the one hand and lower latencies and increased flexibility, manifesting, e.g., in larger messages, on the other.

FlexRay 3.0.1. Due to the complexity of computations, this comparison focuses on the heuristic approaches of conventional and policy-based scheduling. The ILP for policy-based scheduling could only be performed for the first three sets of messages, which have a lower count of periods.

Figure 5.8(b) shows the comparison between the two approaches for FlexRay 3.0.1. The more flexible slot assignment in FlexRay 3.0.1 allows the policy-based scheduling an increase

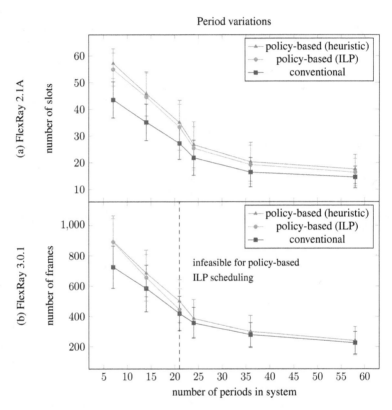

Figure 5.8: *Number of slots and frames required for scheduling with FlexRay 2.1A and FlexRay 3.0.1 for different numbers of periods. Based on the shown performance differences, the typical use cases for the policy-based scheduling would start at 30 different periods and beyond.*

in performance, compared to FlexRay 2.1A. The difference in performance between the conventional and policy-based scheduling falls from 19.1% for the set of periods optimized for conventional FlexRay to 5.7% for a larger selection of periods. These testcases show the potential of the policy-based algorithm. With policy-based scheduling, the user can select any set of periods and is not limited by the communication system. Even non-integer periods are supported by policy-based scheduling, which is not shown here for the sake of comparison to conventional FlexRay.

The flexibility gained by employing the policy-based scheduling approach reduces the design effort for a communication system significantly, as it can be adjusted to the applications. Additionally, the latency is lowered and larger messages sizes can be transmitted. This allows the efficient integration of security frameworks, such as LASAN, the authentication and authorization framework proposed in Chapter 4. The large and infrequent messages can be easily accommodated with policy-based scheduling, while efficient transmission in conventional time-triggered systems is impossible. Policy-based scheduling can also be used in prototyping, when messages in a system change often, as it is not required to always generate a new TDMA schedule, whenever one single message changes.

5.5.4   Computational Performance

As the runtime scheduling of application layer messages to the virtual communication layer is limited to a priority queue, the computational and memory overhead on the ECUs at runtime is minimal. By contrast, the design time scheduling solves the algorithms presented in the previous sections and exhibits varying performance, depending on the FlexRay version and testcase involved. The heuristic approach to policy-based scheduling achieves results in a short amount of time, with the given number of messages per cluster. A FlexRay 2.1A cluster, as shown in this section, can be calculated in about 10 milliseconds, a FlexRay 3.0.1 cluster requires 570 milliseconds on average. The computations have been performed on a workstation with an Intel Xeon quad-core processor with 3.2 GHz and a 64-Bit Java Virtual Machine.

As solver for all policy-based ILPs, SAT4J has been employed [91]. The runtime of the ILP has been limited to 15 minutes for one FlexRay cluster. In case no solution is found within this time frame, the results have been discarded. Due to the higher complexity and exponentially higher number of variables in the ILP for FlexRay 3.0.1 computations, the requirements, especially on the available main memory, are much higher. A high performance computing cluster has been employed to solve these computations, including 4 nodes with 2 Intel Xeon octa-core processors with 2.6 GHz each. The nodes are networked over a 60 Gbps InfiniBand connection and each node contains 192 GB of main memory, allowing to parallelize the computations and boost the main memory available per ILP. We allowed up to 22 GB of main memory for each ILP to achieve the results in this section. This sets the bound for scheduling at 21 periods, as shown in Figure 5.8(b). To schedule a larger set of periods, a larger amount of main memory per ILP process is required. While the performance requirement for the ILP seems high, it is to note that the ILP is only used as a benchmark in this chapter. As shown, the performance of the developed heuristic almost matches the performance of the ILP. Thus, in a production environment, the heuristic would be used, being able to process FlexRay clusters on standard computer equipment within milliseconds.

5.6   Concluding Remarks and Future Work

This chapter proposes a policy-based scheduling mechanism for integration of a virtual event-triggered communication layer into time-triggered communication systems. The policy-based layer is designed to provide asynchronous message transmissions with preemption. In this context, simplified verification of worst-case response times (WCRT) for application layer messages is enabled. A set of algorithms is proposed to schedule policy-based messages in time-triggered systems while ensuring coexistence with existing TDMA communication. An implementation to integrate the proposed approach into the FlexRay static segment has been developed. Based on this implementation, multiple tests have been carried out to evaluate the performance of policy-based FlexRay. The results illustrate a higher flexibility in message size and period selection as well as lower end-to-end latencies with an acceptable trade-off in bandwidth utilization. These elements allow the implementation of security frameworks such as LASAN (see Chapter 4) over time-triggered communication systems, such as FlexRay and thus enable legacy compatibility for in-vehicle security.

Future work comprises the integration with the proposed security framework LASAN. The simulator developed in Chapter 4 shall be extended with FlexRay and policy-based scheduling to allow for simulation of LASAN over policy-based FlexRay. Furthermore, the integration of Audio Video Bridging (AVB) and Time-Sensitive Networking (TSN) with policy-based scheduling for seamless combination of Ethernet and FlexRay bus systems in future in-vehicle communication architectures is targeted.

6

Concluding Remarks

Current automotive E/E architectures have not been designed with security in mind. The increasing amount of connectivity inside and between vehicles and the Internet in recent years made such approaches necessary to ensure the safety of passengers. While gateways to external networks are often protected, internal networks are seldom separated in terms of security. Authentication, authorization and encryption are typically not used and often cannot be employed due to the restriction of the underlying communication systems. Due to the typical bus structure of internal networks, an attacker has full access to all functions, once he penetrated the external gateway. The influence across components is especially high in a bus structure, as all messages could be sent and received by all communication participants. Evaluation this influence and quantifying security in automotive systems is thus not trivial.

While approaches to ensure security in similar areas exist, the combination of low computational power, high security and real-time requirements, influence on safety, and cost are unique in the automotive domain. Especially the influence on safety is important, as it can lead to loss of life in the worst case, e.g. when a vehicle is under attack. A security mechanism exceeding the real-time requirements of the vehicle, can lead to similar consequences. While much work has been performed on securing external interfaces and connections with firewalls and gateway systems, the internal vehicle networks have not received the required attention.

In this thesis, multiple approaches to analysis and design of security in automotive networks are presented. Based on the above requirements, this thesis proposes an analysis mechanisms, allowing to determine the security of in-vehicle systems, as well as an authentication and authorization framework, allowing to efficiently secure the internal communication. Furthermore, addressing the long lifetime of vehicles, a method to integrate security into existing time-triggered vehicle networks, such as FlexRay, is introduced. These main results for each approach are summarized in the following.

Motivated by the lack of existing security evaluation mechanisms for automotive communication system, Security Analysis for Automotive Networks (SAAN) proposes to use probabilistic model checking to evaluate the security of automotive architectures. This evaluation is based on the security assessment of individual components and the interconnections of these components in the form of an architecture. Based on the architecture, a Continuous-Time Markov Chain (CTMC) is synthesized. This CTMC is annotated with the component security scores. Together with a property, defining what part of the architecture is to be analyzed, the model is passed to a probabilistic model checker. The results of the model checking show security aspects of components under the consideration of the complete architecture, such as the time an Electronic Control Unit (ECU) is exploitable. To limit the state space explosion common to model checking, this thesis proposes a model reduction step as part of the model synthesis. This model reduction is based on the specific behavior of automotive communication systems, defined as rules. These rules can reduce the number of states, as well as eliminate unwanted transitions. This leads to a speed-up in the model checking of up to three orders of magnitude. Thus, the model checking can be applied also for larger functions, making it possible to check the security on subsystem level.

While the knowledge of security at design time is important for the network structure, securing traffic at runtime is of similar importance. Authentication frameworks are paramount for this task. Authentication and authorization is required to ensure that every device is who it pretends to be and that only permitted messages are sent. Furthermore, these frameworks can be used to exchange keys securely without any prior knowledge, a prerequisite for encryption of messages. This thesis proposes Lightweight Authentication for Secure Automotive Networks (LASAN), allowing authentication of devices and authorization of messages without affecting the real-time behavior of messages. LASAN is designed for the use in automotive networks. Specifically, the fact that automotive architectures are fixed and only minor changes occur at runtime can be used to optimize existing protocols and reduce message sizes for the use in the automotive domain. This reduces the bandwidth and computation overhead required for traditional authentication frameworks to a minimum. Splitting authentication and authorization, and with this asymmetric and symmetric cryptographic operations, increases worst-case response times further. Evaluations with a newly developed open source simulator for automotive networks show improvements of two to three orders of magnitude over existing frameworks. Additionally, the integration of LASAN with features such as Over-The-Air (OTA) updates and ECU replacement is analyzed. This is important to ensure end-to-end security. The lack of such integration would jeopardize the overall security of the vehicle.

Despite all optimizations, security mechanisms, such as authentication frameworks, still require a large amount of bandwidth, as well as large message sizes. These bandwidth and message requirements are typically less of a problem in upcoming network technologies, such as Controller Area Network (CAN) Flexible Data-Rate (FD) or Automotive Ethernet. In legacy networks, however, implementation can be challenging. Especially in time-triggered networks, such as FlexRay, the assignment of bandwidth to devices is strict to ensure real-time behavior. This thesis proposes to introduce a virtual communication layer into time-triggered networks, adding flexibility to message transmissions. This policy-based message scheduling allows to reduce the cohesion between messages and time slots, while maintaining or even improving worst-case response times. Furthermore, message lengths are no longer limited by the underlying time slots, thus allowing the efficient implementation of security mechanisms, without interference with real-time traffic. It also improves security of conventional messages by increasing the length of encrypted messages and thus hardening the system against brute-force attacks. When employing policy-based scheduling for FlexRay, this thesis shows a reduction of message latencies by nearly one order of magnitude while significantly increasing flexibility in message periods and lengths.

The three approaches to security shown in this thesis are closely linked and form the basis for security in automotive architectures. A flexible message transmission scheme is required to be able to transmit long messages, such as authentication and authorization messages. Enabled on existing and new communication systems, the authentication framework LASAN allows to secure a vehicle network over the complete lifetime of the vehicle. To quantify the security impact by authentication frameworks, such as LASAN, as well as the impact of single components on the architecture, SAAN has been developed. These aspects allow to ensure the security of automotive networks across the complete life cycle of the vehicle. In terms of security, tight integration is of utmost importance, both across time, as well as functions. This thesis presents such approaches.

6.1 Future Work

The approaches to secure automotive E/E architectures in this thesis can only form an initial step into the large area of automotive systems security. Further work is required to ensure the security of automotive architectures and their components. One of the major tasks, both in terms of time and effort, is the standardization of any proposed approach. Only through standardized approaches, it is possible to avoid custom, potentially insecure solutions and enable the clean integration of thoroughly tested approaches. Standardization further fosters widespread adoption of approaches. Thus, it forms the basis of future automotive security solutions.

Furthermore, integration of security is a major challenge. As shown in this thesis, the implications of security mechanisms on real-time behavior and thus, safety-critical behavior of the vehicle, are significant. Integration from the start is thus of high importance. This includes secure coding standards for software in vehicles, a combined safety and security analysis, and control algorithm design incorporating the specifics of security. Some of the integration aspects and their influence on safety-critical systems have been demonstrated in this thesis. This demonstrates that security needs to be seen as a holistic concept in vehicles.

Future secure automotive architectures will also need to include maintenance. While maintaining software is common in many areas of consumer electronics, it is a relatively new field in the automotive domain. Yet, it is highly necessary, especially in terms of security. Even in the most secure systems, security flaws are only discovered over time. The option to patch such security flaws in an efficient manner is paramount for a system ensuring the safety of passengers. Considering the long lifetimes of vehicles on the road increases this demand for timely updates, at least of the security functionality.

In addition to the concerns above, applying to every aspect of the automotive architecture, specifics exist for the individual components. This thesis focuses on the security of the messages and networks in the architecture. Additional work is required in both analysis and design of ECUs. The approaches proposed in this thesis rely on the software on ECUs to be secure. This needs to be ensured with secure (key) storage, secure execution environments, secure boot, etc. Similar to the approaches in this thesis, such approaches exist, but typically do not consider the specifics of automotive networks. Thus, these approaches need to be evaluated and potentially new approaches will be required.

The underlying aspects of encryption also deserve additional attention. This thesis assumes encryption and signing mechanisms as known from the automotive domain. As these are generally considered to be secure, the focus can be on other aspects, such as real-time behavior. However, with lightweight algorithms, targeted towards the automotive domain, the performance of any security measure can be increased significantly. While other algorithms exist, these need to be profiled and evaluated for the use in the automotive domain. Specifically, the influence of small amounts of largely repetitive control data and real-time requirements in control systems pose large challenges to the security algorithms.

Last but not least, the systems designed and constructed, as well as the systems currently on the road, need to be tested. The cryptoanalysis of the separate components of vehicles is largely a manual task. With the increasing amount of interconnections among vehicles, concepts from the domain of design automation can help to reduce the cryptoanalysis of existing systems. Frameworks are required to analyze vehicles, architectures, ECUs, but also maintenance servers and backends in an automated fashion. This area will gain significant focus in the future, similar to the cryptoanalysis existing for consumer devices today. Such efforts in security assessment could mount into a rating system, similar to vehicle safety ratings existing already today.

Besides these technical aspects, large amounts of work are required on the legal and social aspects of vehicle security. Several questions come to mind, e.g.:

- Who is liable in case of a crash, caused by an attack?

- What is required to proof an attack?

- How does the security (rating) of vehicles impact brand recognition?

- Who owns the software in vehicles, is allowed access and alterations?

- What happens to personal data (driving logs, speech recognition data, etc.) generated in vehicles?

- Who controls (copy, delete, etc.) data generated in vehicle?

- Where can data generated from single vehicles or in between vehicle be stored legally?

Much work is required to answer these and similar questions, to establish security in vehicles, and ensure the privacy of owners and passengers. As the decision to buy a vehicle is a highly emotional one, including brand perception and personal aspects, the impact of security on this can form an interesting research topic.

These aspects above are of increasing importance when considering the advent of autonomous vehicles. With increasing autonomy, more control is given to potentially insecure systems. These systems are typically using machine learning to improve their behavior. For this, data is transfered to the Original Equipment Manufacturer (OEM), requiring an Internet connection. This potentially opens access to critical systems for attackers. Security, Privacy and liability questions are of even higher importance in such systems.

This thesis lays the groundwork to answer some of the technical aspects in automotive security. But due to the heterogeneity of OEMs, supply chains, electronic components, networks, legal frameworks, social values, etc. this thesis is a starting point into the area of automotive security. Significant work is required to combine, integrate and ensure security, throughout the design and construction process, throughout the life cycle, and in the minds of the vehicle owners.

Bibliography

[1] ADAC E.V. ADAC deckt Sicherheitslücke auf. https://www.adac.de/infotestrat/adac-im-einsatz/motorwelt/bmw-luecke.aspx, 2015.

[2] ANAND, M., FISCHMEISTER, S., AND LEE, I. A Comparison of Compositional Schedulability Analysis Techniques for Hierarchical Real-time Systems. *ACM Transactions on Embedded Computer Systems 13*, 1 (2013), 2:1–2:37.

[3] APPLE. CarPlay. http://www.apple.com/ios/carplay. Accessed: 2016-01-19.

[4] ARGUS CYBER SECURITY. Argus Solutions. http://argus-sec.com/solutions, 2016. Accessed: 2016-01-06.

[5] ARM LIMITED. TrustZone. http://www.arm.com/products/processors/technologies/trustzone, 2016. Accessed: 2016-01-18.

[6] AUTOMATIC LABS. Automatic: Connect Your Car To Your Life. https://www.automatic.com, 2015. Accessed: 2016-01-19.

[7] AUTOMOTIVE OPEN SYSTEM ARCHITECTURE (AUTOSAR). Requirements on Module Secure Onboard Communication, 2015. Version 4.2.2.

[8] AUTOMOTIVE OPEN SYSTEM ARCHITECTURE (AUTOSAR). Specification of Crypto Abstraction Library, 2015. Version 4.2.2.

[9] AUTOMOTIVE OPEN SYSTEM ARCHITECTURE (AUTOSAR). Specification of Module Secure Onboard Communication, 2015. Version 4.2.2.

[10] BASAGIANNIS, S., KATSAROS, P., POMBORTSIS, A., AND ALEXIOU, N. Probabilistic model checking for the quantification of DoS security threats. *Computers & Security 28*, 6 (2009), 450–465.

[11] BEN OTHMANE, L., FERNANDO, R., RANCHAL, R., BHARGAVA, B., AND BODDEN, E. Likelihood of Threats to Connected Vehicles. *International Journal of Next-Generation Computing (IJNGC) 5*, 3 (2014).

[12] BERNSTEIN, D. J. Circuits for Integer Factorization: A Proposal. https://cr.yp.to/papers/nfscircuit.pdf, 2011.

[13] BERNSTEIN, D. J., AND LANGE, T. SafeCurves: choosing safe curves for elliptic-curve cryptography. http://safecurves.cr.yp.to, 2014. Accessed: 2016-01-18.

[14] BUGCROWD. Tesla Motors. https://bugcrowd.com/tesla, 2015.

[15] CHECKOWAY, S., McCOY, D., KANTOR, B., ANDERSON, D., SHACHAM, H., SAVAGE, S., KOSCHER, K., CZESKIS, A., ROESNER, F., AND KOHNO, T. Comprehensive experimental analyses of automotive attack surfaces. In *Proceedings of USENIX Security* (2011).

[16] CLAESSON, V., AND SURI, N. TTET: event-triggered channels on a time-triggered base.

[17] COOPER, D., SANTESSON, S., FARRELL, S., BOEYEN, S., HOUSLEY, R., AND POLK, W. *RFC 5280: Internet X.509 Public Key Infrastructure Certificate and Certificate Revocation List (CRL) Profile*. Request for Comments. IETF, 2008.

[18] CREMERS, C. J. F. The Scyther Tool: Verification, Falsification, and Analysis of Security Protocols. In *Computer Aided Verification*, no. 5123 in Lecture Notes in Computer Science. Springer Berlin Heidelberg, 2008, pp. 414–418.

[19] CREMERS, C. J. F. Unbounded verification, falsification, and characterization of security protocols by pattern refinement. In *CCS '08: Proceedings of the 15th ACM conference on Computer and communications security* (2008), pp. 119–128.

[20] DAVIS, R. I., BURNS, A., BRIL, R. J., AND LUKKIEN, J. J. Controller Area Network (CAN) schedulability analysis: Refuted, revisited and revised. *Real-Time Systems 35*, 3 (2007), 239–272.

[21] DENNING, D. E. An Intrusion-Detection Model. In *Proceedings of the 1986 IEEE Symposium on Security and Privacy (SP)* (USA, 1986), pp. 118–131.

[22] DI NATALE, M., AND SANGIOVANNI-VINCENTELLI, A. Moving From Federated to Integrated Architectures in Automotive: The Role of Standards, Methods and Tools. *Proceedings of the IEEE 98*, 4 (2010), 603–620.

[23] DIERKS, T., AND RESCORLA, E. *RFC 5246: The Transport Layer Security (TLS) Protocol Version 1.2*. Request for Comments. IETF, 2008.

[24] DOLEV, D., AND YAO, A. C. On the Security of Public Key Protocols. In *Proceedings of the 22nd Annual Symposium on Foundations of Computer Science* (1981), SFCS '81, pp. 350–357.

[25] DU, H., AND YANG, S. Probabilistic inference for obfuscated network attack sequences. In *2014 44th Annual IEEE/IFIP International Conference on Dependable Systems and Networks (DSN)* (2014), pp. 57–67.

[26] DWORKIN, M. *Recommendation for Block Cipher Modes of Operation: The CMAC Mode for Authentication.* NIST Special Publication 800-38B. United States National Institute of Standards and Technology (NIST), 2005.

[27] EASWARAN, A., SHIN, I., SOKOLSKY, O., AND LEE, I. Incremental Schedulability Analysis of Hierarchical Real-time Components. In *Proceedings of the 6th ACM & IEEE International Conference on Embedded Software* (USA, 2006), EMSOFT '06, pp. 272–281.

[28] EDILOCK GROUP LTD. Automotive Software Developing. http://www.vag-info.com, 2016. Accessed: 2016-01-07.

[29] ENVIRONMENTAL PROTECTION AGENCY. *Control of Air Pollution From New Motor Vehicles and New Motor Vehicle Engines; Modification of Federal On-Board Diagnostic Regulations for: Light-Duty Vehicles, Light-Duty Trucks, Medium Duty Passenger Vehicles, Complete Heavy Duty Vehicles and Engines Intended for Use in Heavy Duty Vehicles Weighing 14,000 Pounds GVWR or Less.* 2005.

[30] ESCHERICH, R., LEDENDECKER, I., SCHMAL, C., KUHLS, B., GROTHE, C., AND SCHARBERTH, F. *SHE – Secure Hardware Extension Functional Specification.* 2009.

[31] EUROPEAN UNION. *Directive 98/69/EC of the European Parliament and of the Council of 13 October 1998 relating to measures to be taken against air pollution by emissions from motor vehicles and amending Council Directive 70/220/EEC.* 1998.

[32] FAQIH, M. Isi Baterai 15 Menit, Taksi Ini Dapat Menempuh 200 Km. http://www.republika.co.id/berita/otomotif/mobil/13/11/27/mwx57y-isi-baterai-15-menit-taksi-ini-dapat-menempuh-200-km, 2013. Republika.

[33] FEDERAL MINISTRY OF TRANSPORT AND DIGITAL INFRASTRUCTURE. Strategie automatisiertes und vernetztes Fahren. http://www.bmvi.de/SharedDocs/DE/Publikationen/StB/broschuere-strategie-automatisiertes-vernetztes-fahren.pdf?__blob=publicationFile, 2015. Germany. Accessed: 2016-01-19.

[34] FOSTER, I., PRUDHOMME, A., KOSCHER, A., AND SAVAGE, S. Fast and Vulnerable: A Story of Telematic Failures. In *9th USENIX Workshop on Offensive Technologies (WOOT 15)* (USA, 2015).

[35] FOX, B. L., AND GLYNN, P. W. Computing Poisson Probabilities. *Commun. ACM 31*, 4 (1988), 440–445.

[36] FRANCILLON, A., DANEV, B., AND CAPKUN, S. Relay Attacks on Passive Keyless Entry and Start Systems in Modern Cars. In *Proceedings of the Network and Distributed System Security Symposium (NDSS)* (2011).

[37] GOOGLE. Android Auto. https://www.android.com/auto. Accessed: 2016-01-19.

[38] GRENIER, M., HAVET, L., AND NAVET, N. Configuring the communication on FlexRay-the case of the static segment.

[39] GROZA, B., MURVAY, S., VAN HERREWEGE, A., AND VERBAUWHEDE, I. LiBrA-CAN: A Lightweight Broadcast Authentication Protocol for Controller Area Networks. In *Cryptology and Network Security*, Lecture Notes in Computer Science. 2012, pp. 185–200.

[40] HACKERONE. General Motors. https://hackerone.com/gm, 2015.

[41] HAMDAOUI, M., AND RAMANATHAN, P. A service policy for real-time customers with (m, k) firm deadlines. pp. 196–205.

[42] HAN, G., ZENG, H., LI, Y., AND DOU, W. SAFE: Security-Aware FlexRay Scheduling Engine. In *Design, Automation and Test in Europe Conference and Exhibition (DATE)* (2014), pp. 1–4.

[43] HAO, J., WU, J., AND GUO, C. Modeling and simulation of CAN network based on OPNET. In *IEEE 3rd International Conference on Communication Software and Networks (ICCSN 2011)* (China, 2011), pp. 577–581.

[44] HERBER, C., RICHTER, A., WILD, T., AND HERKERSDORF, A. A network virtualization approach for performance isolation in controller area network (CAN). In *20th IEEE Real-Time and Embedded Technology and Applications Symposium (RTAS)* (2014), pp. 215–224.

[45] HOPPE, T., KILTZ, S., AND DITTMANN, J. Adaptive Dynamic Reaction to Automotive IT Security Incidents Using Multimedia Car Environment. In *Fourth International Conference on Information Assurance and Security (ISIAS)* (2008), pp. 295–298.

[46] HOPPE, T., KILTZ, S., AND DITTMANN, J. Security threats to automotive CAN networks—Practical examples and selected short-term countermeasures. *Reliability Engineering & System Safety 96*, 1 (2011), 11–25.

[47] IEC - INTERNATIONAL ELECTROTECHNICAL COMMISSION. IEC 62443-1-1:2009 Industrial communication networks - Network and system security - Part 1-1: Terminology, concepts and models, 2009.

[48] IEC - INTERNATIONAL ELECTROTECHNICAL COMMISSION. IEC 62443-3-3:2013 Industrial communication networks - Network and system security - Part 3-3: System security requirements and security levels, 2013.

[49] IEC - INTERNATIONAL ELECTROTECHNICAL COMMISSION. IEC 61158-1:2014 Industrial communication networks - Fieldbus specifications - Part 1: Overview and guidance for the IEC 61158 and IEC 61784 series, 2014.

[50] INCHRON GMBH. chronSIM. http://www.inchron.com/tool-suite/chronsim.html, 2015. Accessed: 2015-11-23.

[51] INSTITUTE OF ELECTRICAL AND ELECTRONICS ENGINEERS (IEEE). IEEE 802.1BA-2011 PDF format IEEE Standard for Local and metropolitan area networks–Audio Video Bridging (AVB) Systems, 2011.

[52] INSTITUTE OF ELECTRICAL AND ELECTRONICS ENGINEERS (IEEE). IEEE 802.3-2012 – IEEE Standard for Ethernet, 2012.

[53] INSTITUTE OF ELECTRICAL AND ELECTRONICS ENGINEERS (IEEE). IEEE 802.1Q-2014 IEEE Standard for Local and metropolitan area networks–Bridges and Bridged Networks, 2014.

[54] INSTITUTE OF ELECTRICAL AND ELECTRONICS ENGINEERS (IEEE). IEEE P802.3bp 1000BASE-T1 PHY Task Force. http://www.ieee802.org/3/bp, 2014. Accessed: 2016-01-18.

[55] INSTITUTE OF ELECTRICAL AND ELECTRONICS ENGINEERS (IEEE). IEEE P802.3bw 100BASE-T1 Task Force. http://www.ieee802.org/3/bw, 2015. Accessed: 2016-01-18.

[56] INSTITUTE OF ELECTRICAL AND ELECTRONICS ENGINEERS (IEEE). Time-Sensitive Networking Task Group. http://www.ieee802.org/1/pages/tsn.html, 2015. Accessed: 2016-01-18.

[57] ISO - INTERNATIONAL ORGANIZATION FOR STANDARDIZATION. ISO 11898-1:2003 Road vehicles – Controller area network (CAN) – Part 1: Data link layer and physical signalling, 2003.

[58] ISO - INTERNATIONAL ORGANIZATION FOR STANDARDIZATION. ISO 11898-2:2003 Road vehicles – Controller area network (CAN) – Part 2: High-speed medium access unit, 2003.

[59] ISO - INTERNATIONAL ORGANIZATION FOR STANDARDIZATION. ISO 11898-3:2006 Road vehicles – Controller area network (CAN) – Part 3: Low-speed, fault-tolerant, medium-dependent interface, 2006.

[60] ISO - INTERNATIONAL ORGANIZATION FOR STANDARDIZATION. ISO/IEC 15408-2:2008 Information technology – Security techniques – Evaluation criteria for IT security – Part 2: Security functional components, 2008.

[61] ISO - INTERNATIONAL ORGANIZATION FOR STANDARDIZATION. ISO/IEC 15408-3:2008 Information technology – Security techniques – Evaluation criteria for IT security – Part 3: Security assurance components, 2008.

[62] ISO - INTERNATIONAL ORGANIZATION FOR STANDARDIZATION. ISO/IEC 11889-1:2009 information technology – trusted platform module – part 1: Overview.

[63] ISO - INTERNATIONAL ORGANIZATION FOR STANDARDIZATION. ISO/IEC 15408-1:2009 Information technology – Security techniques – Evaluation criteria for IT security – Part 1: Introduction and general model, 2009.

[64] ISO - INTERNATIONAL ORGANIZATION FOR STANDARDIZATION. ISO/IEC 18033-3:2010 Information technology – Security techniques – Encryption algorithms – Part 3: Block ciphers, 2010.

[65] ISO - INTERNATIONAL ORGANIZATION FOR STANDARDIZATION. ISO 13400-3:2011 Road vehicles — Diagnostic communication over Internet Protocol (DoIP) — Part 3: Wired vehicle interface based on IEEE 802.3, 2011.

[66] ISO - INTERNATIONAL ORGANIZATION FOR STANDARDIZATION. ISO 15765-2:2011 Road vehicles – Diagnostic communication over Controller Area Network (DoCAN) – Part 2: Transport protocol and network layer services, 2011.

[67] ISO - INTERNATIONAL ORGANIZATION FOR STANDARDIZATION. ISO 26262-1:2011 Road vehicles – Functional safety – Part 1: Vocabulary, 2011.

[68] ISO - INTERNATIONAL ORGANIZATION FOR STANDARDIZATION. ISO 26262-10:2012 Road vehicles – Functional safety – Part 10: Guideline on ISO 26262, 2012.

[69] ISO - INTERNATIONAL ORGANIZATION FOR STANDARDIZATION. ISO 17458-1:2013 Road vehicles – FlexRay communications system – Part 1: General information and use case definition, 2013.

[70] ISO - INTERNATIONAL ORGANIZATION FOR STANDARDIZATION. ISO 17458-2:2013 Road vehicles – FlexRay communications system – Part 2: Data link layer specification, 2013.

[71] ISO - INTERNATIONAL ORGANIZATION FOR STANDARDIZATION. ISO 17458-3:2013 Road vehicles – FlexRay communications system – Part 3: Data link layer conformance test specification, 2013.

[72] ISO - INTERNATIONAL ORGANIZATION FOR STANDARDIZATION. ISO 17458-4:2013 Road vehicles – FlexRay communications system – Part 4: Electrical physical layer specification, 2013.

[73] ISO - INTERNATIONAL ORGANIZATION FOR STANDARDIZATION. ISO 17458-5:2013 Road vehicles – FlexRay communications system – Part 5: Electrical physical layer conformance test specification, 2013.

[74] ISO - INTERNATIONAL ORGANIZATION FOR STANDARDIZATION. ISO/IEC 27001:2013 Information technology – Security techniques – Information security management systems – Requirements, 2013.

[75] ISO - INTERNATIONAL ORGANIZATION FOR STANDARDIZATION. ISO/IEC 27002:2013 Information technology – Security techniques – Code of practice for information security controls, 2013.

[76] ISO - INTERNATIONAL ORGANIZATION FOR STANDARDIZATION. ISO 11898-1:2015 Road vehicles – Controller area network (CAN) – Part 1: Data link layer and physical signalling, 2015.

[77] ISO - INTERNATIONAL ORGANIZATION FOR STANDARDIZATION. ISO/TC 22/SC 31 Data communication. http://www.iso.org/iso/home/standards_development/list_of_iso_technical_committees/iso_technical_committee.htm?commid=5383568, 2016. Accessed: 2016-01-18.

[78] ISSARIYAKUL, T., AND HOSSAIN, E. *Introduction to Network Simulator NS2*. 2008.

[79] JIANG, K., ELES, P., AND PENG, Z. Co-design techniques for distributed real-time embedded systems with communication security constraints. In *Design, Automation Test in Europe Conference Exhibition (DATE)* (2012), pp. 947–952.

[80] KAMKAR, S. Drive It Like You Hacked It: New Attacks and Tools to Wirelessly Steal Cars. In *Proceedings of DEF CON* (2015).

[81] KARGL, F. Secure Vehicle Communication (SeVeCom) - Baseline Security Specification, 2009.

[82] KING, D. Eva electric taxi concept geared for tropical cities, cools your head. http://www.autoblog.com/2013/11/26/eva-electric-taxi-concept-geared-for-tropical-cities-cools-your, 2013. autoblog.

[83] KOPETZ, H., AND BAUER, G. The Time-Triggered Architecture. vol. 91, pp. 112–126.

[84] KOPETZ, H., AND GRUNSTEIDL, G. TTP - A protocol for fault-tolerant real-time systems. *Computer 27*, 1 (1994), 14–23.

[85] KOSCHER, K., CZESKIS, A., ROESNER, F., PATEL, S., KOHNO, T., CHECKOWAY, S., MCCOY, D., KANTOR, B., ANDERSON, D., SHACHAM, H., AND SAVAGE, S. Experimental Security Analysis of a Modern Automobile. In *Proceedings of Symposium on Security and Privacy (SP)* (2010), pp. 447–462.

[86] KWIATKOWSKA, M., NORMAN, G., AND PARKER, D. Stochastic Model Checking. In *Formal Methods for Performance Evaluation*, no. 4486 in Lecture Notes in Computer Science. 2007, pp. 220–270.

[87] KWIATKOWSKA, M., NORMAN, G., AND PARKER, D. PRISM 4.0: Verification of Probabilistic Real-time Systems. In *Proceedings of the 23rd International Conference on Computer Aided Verification* (2011), vol. 6806, pp. 585–591.

[88] LANGE, R., AND VASQUES, F. Guaranteeing real-time message deadlines in the FlexRay static segment using a on-line scheduling approach. pp. 301–310.

[89] LANGHAMMER, A. E-Taxi für Singapur. http://www.autobild.de/artikel/elektro-taxi-eva-tokyo-motor-show-2013-4461235.html, 2013. Auto Bild.

[90] LAURIE, B., LANGLEY, A., AND KASPER, E. *RFC 6962: Certificate Transparency.* Request for Comments. IETF, 2013.

[91] LE BERRE, D., AND PARRAIN, A. The SAT4J library, Release 2.2, System Description. *Journal on Satisfiability, Boolean Modeling and Computation 7* (2010), 59–64.

[92] LE BOUDEC, J., AND THIRAN, P. *Network Calculus: A Theory of Deterministic Queuing Systems for the Internet.* 2001.

[93] LEURENT, T. TUM CREATE EVA - Un taxi électrique au salon de Tokyo. http://www.avem.fr/actualite-tum-create-eva-un-taxi-electrique-au-salon-de-tokyo-4598.html, 2013.

[94] LIN, C., ZHU, Q., PHUNG, C., AND SANGIOVANNI-VINCENTELLI, A. Security-aware mapping for CAN-based real-time distributed automotive systems. In *2013 IEEE/ACM International Conference on Computer-Aided Design (ICCAD)* (2013), pp. 115–121.

[95] LOWE, G. Towards a completeness result for model checking of security protocols. *Journal of Computer Security 7*, 2 (1999), 89–146.

[96] LUKASIEWYCZ, M., GLASS, M., MILBREDT, P., AND TEICH, J. FlexRay Schedule Optimization of the Static Segment. In *Proceedings of the 7th IEEE/ACM International Conference on Hardware/Software Codesign and System Synthesis (CODES+ISSS)* (2009), vol. 9, pp. 363–372.

[97] LUKASIEWYCZ, M., MUNDHENK, P., AND STEINHORST, S. Security-aware Obfuscated Priority Assignment for Automotive CAN Platforms. *ACM Transactions on Design Automation of Electronic Systems (TODAES) 21*, 2 (2016), 32:1–32:27.

[98] MAIER, R. Event-triggered communication on top of time-triggered architecture. In *Proceedings of the 21st Digital Avionics Systems Conference* (2002), pp. 13C5–1 – 13C5–9.

[99] MANIMARAN, G., SHASHIDHAR, M., MANIKUTTY, A., AND MURTHY, C. S. R. Integrated scheduling of tasks and messages in distributed real-time systems. pp. 64–71.

[100] MARKEY, E. J. S.1806 - Security and Privacy in Your Car Act of 2015. https://www.congress.gov/bill/114th-congress/senate-bill/1806, 2015. Accessed: 2016-01-19.

[101] MARKEY, E. J. Tracking & Hacking: Security & Privacy Gaps Put American Drivers at Risk, 2015.

[102] MATSUMURA, J., MATSUBARA, Y., TAKADA, H., OI, M., TOYOSHIMA, M., AND IWAI, A. A Simulation Environment based on OMNeT++ for Automotive CAN–Ethernet Networks. In *Proceedings of the 4th International Workshop on Analysis Tools and Methodologies for Embedded and Real-time Systems (WATERS 2013)* (France, 2013).

[103] MAURER, M., AND WINNER, H. *Automotive Systems Engineering*. Springer-Verlag Berlin Heidelberg, 2013.

[104] METROMILE INC. Metromile: Pay-per-mile insurance & smart driving app. https://www.metromile.com, 2015. Accessed: 2016-01-19.

[105] MILLER, C., AND VALASEK, C. Adventures in Automotive Networks and Control Units. In *Proceedings of DEF CON* (2013).

[106] MILLER, C., AND VALASEK, C. A Survey of Remote Automotive Attack Surfaces. In *Proceedings of Black Hat* (2014).

[107] MILLER, C., AND VALASEK, C. Remote Exploitation of an Unaltered Passenger Vehicle. In *Proceedings of Black Hat* (2015).

[108] MOREAUX, J. Data transmission system for aircraft. http://worldwide.espacenet.com/publicationDetails/biblio?CC=US&NR=6925088, 2005. US Patent 6925088.

[109] MOST COOPERATION. MOST Cooperation: Specifications & Organizational Procedures. http://www.mostcooperation.com/publications/specifications-organizational-procedures/, 2016. Accessed: 2016-01-18.

[110] MUNDHENK, P. Online repository for PulseAudioJava. https://github.com/ PhilippMundhenk/PulseAudioJava, 2016.

[111] MUNDHENK, P., MROWCA, A., STEINHORST, S., LUKASIEWYCZ, M., FAHMY, S. A., AND CHAKRABORTY, S. Open Source Model and Simulator for Real-Time Performance Analysis of Automotive Network Security. *SIGBED Review 13*, 3 (2016), 8–13.

[112] MUNDHENK, P., PAVERD, A., MROWCA, A., STEINHORST, S., LUKASIEWYCZ, M., FAHMY, S. A., AND CHAKRABORTY, S. System Level Design Approaches to Security in Automotive Networks. *ACM Transactions on Design Automation of Electronic Systems 22*, 2 (2017), 25:1–25:27.

[113] MUNDHENK, P., SAGSTETTER, F., STEINHORST, S., LUKASIEWYCZ, M., AND CHAKRABORTY, S. Policy-based Message Scheduling Using FlexRay. In *Proceedings of the 12th International Conference on Hardware/Software Codesign and System Synthesis (CODES+ISSS)* (India, 2014), pp. 19:1–19:10.

[114] MUNDHENK, P., STEINHORST, S., LUKASIEWYCZ, M., FAHMY, S. A., AND CHAKRABORTY, S. Lightweight Authentication for Secure Automotive Networks. In *Proceedings of the Conference on Design, Automation and Test in Europe (DATE)* (France, 2015), pp. 285–288.

[115] MUNDHENK, P., STEINHORST, S., LUKASIEWYCZ, M., FAHMY, S. A., AND CHAKRABORTY, S. Security Analysis of Automotive Architectures using Probabilistic Model Checking. In *Proceedings of the 52nd Design Automation Conference (DAC)* (USA, 2015), pp. 38:1–38:6.

[116] MUTER, M., AND ASAJ, N. Entropy-based anomaly detection for in-vehicle networks. In *2011 IEEE Intelligent Vehicles Symposium (IV)* (2011), pp. 1110–1115.

[117] NATIONAL INSTITUTE OF STANDARDS AND TECHNOLOGY (NIST). Federal information processing standards publication (FIPS 46-3). Data Encryption Standard (DES). http://csrc.nist.gov/publications/fips/fips46-3/fips46-3.pdf, 1999.

[118] NEUKIRCHNER, M., NEGREAN, M., ERNST, R., AND BONE, T. Response-time analysis of the flexray dynamic segment under consideration of slot-multiplexing. In *7th IEEE International Symposium on Industrial Embedded Systems (SIES)* (2012), pp. 21–30.

[119] NEUMAN, C., YU, T., HARTMAN, S., AND RAEBURN, K. *RFC 4120: The Kerberos Network Authentication Service (V5)*. Request for Comments. IETF, 2005.

[120] NIST. *Specification for the Advanced Encryption Standard (AES)*. Federal Information Processing Standards Publication 197. United States National Institute of Standards and Technology (NIST), 2001.

[121] NVIDIA CORPORATION. NVIDIA Tegra® X1. http://www.nvidia.com/object/tegra-x1-processor.html, 2016. Accessed: 2016-01-15.

[122] NXP SEMICONDUCTORS. 8-bit S08 5.5V MCUs. http://www.nxp.com/products/automotive-products/microcontrollers-and-processors/8-bit-s08-5.5v-mcus, 2016. Accessed: 2016-01-15.

[123] NXP SEMICONDUCTORS. i.MX35 Applications Processors based on ARM11™ Core. http://www.nxp.com/products/microcontrollers-and-processors/arm-processors/i.mx-applications-processors-based-on-arm-cores/i.mx35-processors, 2016. Accessed: 2016-01-15.

[124] OBERMAISSER, R. End-to-End Delays of Event-Triggered Overlay Networks in a Time-Triggered Architecture. pp. 541–546.

[125] OFIR, R., AND KAPOTA, O. A remote attack on an aftermarket telematics service. http://argus-sec.com/blog/remote-attack-aftermarket-telematics-service, 2014. Accessed: 2016-01-19.

[126] OH, C. Made in Singapore: Fast-charging electric taxi launched. http://www.channelnewsasia.com/news/technology/made-in-singapore-fast/1804176.html, 2015. Channel News Asia.

[127] OPEN ALLIANCE. BroadR-Reach® Specifications. http://www.opensig.org/about/specifications, 2016. Accessed: 2016-01-18.

[128] OSSWALD, S., ZEHE, D., MUNDHENK, P., SHETH, P., SCHALLER, M., SCHICKRAM, S., AND GLEYZES, D. HMI Development for a Purpose-Built Electric Taxi in Singapore. In *Proceedings of the International Conference on Human-Computer Interaction with Mobile Devices and Services, MobileHCI '13* (2013), pp. 434–439.

[129] OZDOGAN, B. 15 dakika şarjla 200 km gidebilen elektrikli taksi. http://www.log.com.tr/15-dakika-sarjla-200-km-gidebilen-elektrikli-taksi, 2013. Log.

[130] PANDER, J. E-Taxi für schwüle Megacities: Ohne Schweiß, billiger Preis. http://www.spiegel.de/auto/aktuell/elektrotaxi-eva-fuer-tropische-megacities-a-1032824.html, 2015. Spiegel Online.

[131] PAVERD, A., AND MARTIN, A. Hardware Security for Device Authentication in the Smart Grid. In *First Open EIT ICT Labs Workshop on Smart Grid Security - SmartGrid-Sec12* (Germany, 2012), pp. 72–84.

[132] PAVERD, A. J., MARTIN, A. P., AND BROWN, I. Privacy-Enhanced Bi-Directional Communication in the Smart Grid using Trusted Computing. In *Fifth IEEE International Conference on Smart Grid Communications (SmartGridComm)* (2014), pp. 872–877.

[133] PERRIG, A., SONG, D., CANETTI, R., TYGAR, J. D., AND BRISCOE, B. *RFC 4082: Timed Efficient Stream Loss-Tolerant Authentication (TESLA): Multicast Source Authentication Transform Introduction.* Request for Comments. IETF, 2005.

[134] POULSEN, K. Hacker Disables More Than 100 Cars Remotely. http://www.wired.com/2010/03/hacker-bricks-cars/, 2010.

[135] PROGRESSIVE CASUALTY INSURANCE COMPANY. Snapshot®. https://www.progressive.com/auto/snapshot, 2016. Accessed: 2016-01-19.

[136] QNX SOFTWARE SYSTEMS LIMITED. QNX operating systems, development tools, and professional services for connected embedded systems. http://www.qnx.com/, 2016. Accessed: 2016-01-18.

[137] RENESAS ELECTRONICS CORPORATION. RH850/D1M. http://www.renesas.com/products/mpumcu/rh850/rh850d1x/rh850d1m/index.jsp, 2016. Accessed: 2016-01-15.

[138] RENESAS ELECTRONICS CORPORATION. RL78/F1x. http://www.renesas.com/products/mpumcu/rl78/rl78f1x/index.jsp, 2016. Accessed: 2016-01-15.

[139] RIBBENS, W. B. *Understanding Automotive Electronics (Sixth Edition)*, 6 ed. Newnes, 2003.

[140] RITCHEY, R., AND AMMANN, P. Using model checking to analyze network vulnerabilities. In *Proceedings of the IEEE Symposium on Security and Privacy (SP)* (2000), pp. 156–165.

[141] RIVERBED TECHNOLOGY. Riverbed modeler. http://www.riverbed.com/products/steelcentral/steelcentral-riverbed-modeler.html, 2015. Accessed: 2015-10-12.

[142] ROBERT BOSCH GMBH. *Bosch Automotive Electrics and Automotive Electronics*, 5 ed. Bosch Professional Automotive Information. Springer Vieweg, 2014.

[143] RSA LABORATORIES. PKCS #1 v2.2: RSA Cryptography Standard. http://www.emc.com/emc-plus/rsa-labs/pkcs/files/h11300-wp-pkcs-1v2-2-rsa-cryptography-standard.pdf, 2012.

[144] SAE INTERNATIONAL. Cybersecurity Guidebook for Cyber-Physical Vehicle Systems, 2016.

[145] SAGSTETTER, F., LUKASIEWYCZ, M., STEINHORST, S., WOLF, M., BOUARD, A., HARRIS, W. R., JHA, S., PEYRIN, T., POSCHMANN, A., AND CHAKRABORTY, S. Security challenges in automotive hardware/software architecture design. In *Design, Automation Test in Europe Conference Exhibition (DATE)* (2013), pp. 458–463.

[146] SANTESSON, S., MYERS, M., ANKNEY, R., MALPANI, A., GALPERIN, S., AND ADAMS, C. *RFC 6960: X.509 Internet Public Key Infrastructure - Online Certificate Status Protocol - OCSP*. Request for Comments. IETF, 2013.

[147] SCHÄUFFELE, J., AND ZURAWKA, T. *Automotive Software Engineering*. SAE International, 2005.

[148] SCHIFFMAN, M., ESCHELBECK, G., AHMAD, D., AND ROMANOSKY, S. *CVSS: A Common Vulnerability Scoring System*. National Infrastructure Advisory Council (NIAC), 2004.

[149] SCHMIDT, E. G., AND SCHMIDT, K. Schedulability Analysis and Message Schedule Computation for the Dynamic Segment of FlexRay. pp. 1–5.

[150] SCHMIDT, K., AND SCHMIDT, E. G. Message Scheduling for the FlexRay Protocol : The Static Segment. *IEEE Transactions on Vehicular Technology 58*, 5 (2009), 2170–2179.

[151] SCHMIDT, K., AND SCHMIDT, E. G. Optimal Message Scheduling for the Static Segment of FlexRay. In *IEEE 72nd Vehicular Technology Conference Fall (VTC)* (2010).

[152] SEUDIÉ, H. Vehicular On-board Security: EVITA Project, 2009.

[153] SHREEJITH, S., AND FAHMY, S. A. Zero latency encryption with FPGAs for secure time-triggered automotive networks. In *2014 International Conference on Field-Programmable Technology (FPT)* (2014), pp. 256–259.

[154] SHREEJITH, S., AND FAHMY, S. A. Security aware network controllers for next generation automotive embedded systems. In *Proceedings of the 52nd Design Automation Conference (DAC)* (USA, 2015), pp. 39:1–39:6.

[155] SIKORA, A. Architecture and Development of Secure Communication Solutions for Smart Grid Applications. *Journal of Communications (JCM) 8*, 8 (2013), 490–496.

[156] SIMON TOUCH. Key Prog Tools. http://www.keyprogtools.com, 2016. Accessed: 2016-01-07.

[157] SMITH, D. C. Federal Motor Vehicle Safety Standards: Vehicle-to-Vehicle (V2V) Communications. http://www.nhtsa.gov/staticfiles/rulemaking/pdf/V2V/V2V-ANPRM_081514.pdf, 2014. United States Department of Transportation - National Highway Traffic Safety Administration (NHTSA).

[158] SOJKA, M., KREC, M., AND HANZALEK, Z. Case study on combined validation of safety & security requirements. In *2014 9th IEEE International Symposium on Industrial Embedded Systems (SIES)* (2014), pp. 244–251.

[159] STANDARDS FOR EFFICIENT CRYPTOGRAPHY GROUP (SECG). SEC 1: Elliptic Curve Cryptography Version 2.0. http://www.secg.org/sec1-v2.pdf, 2009.

[160] STANDARDS FOR EFFICIENT CRYPTOGRAPHY GROUP (SECG). SEC 2: Recommended Elliptic Curve Domain Parameters Version 2.0. http://www.secg.org/sec2-v2.pdf, 2010.

[161] STEINHORST, S., LUKASIEWYCZ, M., NARAYANASWAMY, S., KAUER, M., AND CHAKRABORTY, S. Smart Cells for Embedded Battery Management. In *Proceedings of the 2014 IEEE International Conference on Cyber-Physical Systems, Networks, and Applications (CPSNA)* (Hong Kong, 2014), pp. 59–64.

[162] SUH, G. E., AND DEVADAS, S. Physical unclonable functions for device authentication and secret key generation. In *Proceedings of the 44th Annual Design Automation Conference (DAC)* (USA, 2007).

[163] SYMTAVISION GMBH. SymTA/S & Trace Analyzer. https://www.symtavision.com/products/symtas-traceanalyzer, 2015. Accessed: 2015-11-23.

[164] TEAM SIMPY. SimPy Discrete Event Simulation Library for Python. http://simpy.readthedocs.org, 2015. Accessed: 2015-04-20.

[165] THIELE, L., CHAKRABORTY, S., AND NAEDELE, M. Real-time calculus for scheduling hard real-time systems. In *Proceedings of the 2000 IEEE International Symposium on Circuits and Systems (ISCAS)* (Switzerland, 2000), pp. 101–104.

[166] THUEN, C. S4x15 Video – Remote Control Automobiles. http://www.digitalbond.com/blog/2015/02/02/s4x15-video-remote-control-automobiles, 2015. Accessed: 2016-01-19.

[167] TIMING-ARCHITECTS EMBEDDED SYSTEMS GMBH. Simulator. http://www.timing-architects.com/ta-tool-suite/simulator, 2015. Accessed: 2015-11-23.

[168] TINDELL, K., BURNS, A., AND WELLINGS, A. J. Calculating controller area network (CAN) message response times. *Control Engineering Practice* (1995).

[169] TISCALI:MOTORI. Arriva EVA, il taxi che fa 200 km con 15 minuti di ricarica. http://motori.tiscali.it/feeds/13/12/09/t_70_20131209_news_900388.html, 2013.

[170] TOWERSEC. ECUSHIELD. http://tower-sec.com/ecushield, 2016. Accessed: 2016-01-06.

[171] TUM CREATE. EVA by TUM CREATE - Electric Taxi for Tropical Megacities. http://www.eva-taxi.sg/, 2013.

[172] TYAN, H., AND HOU, J. C. A rate-based message scheduling paradigm. In *Proceedings of the Fourth International Workshop on Object-Oriented Real-Time Dependable Systems* (1999), pp. 203–215.

[173] VAN HERREWEGE, A., SINGELEE, D., AND VERBAUWHEDE, I. CANAuth - A Simple, Backward Compatible Broadcast Authentication Protocol for CAN bus. In *ECRYPT Workshop on Lightweight Cryptography 2011* (2011).

[174] VARGA, A., AND HORNIG, R. An Overview of the OMNeT++ Simulation Environment. In *Proceedings of the 1st International Conference on Simulation Tools and Techniques for Communications, Networks and Systems & Workshops* (France, 2008), pp. 60:1–60:10.

[175] VERDULT, R., GARCIA, F. D., AND EGE, B. Dismantling megamos crypto: Wirelessly lockpicking a vehicle immobilizer. In *22nd USENIX Security Symposium (USENIX Security)* (2015), USENIX Association, pp. 703–718.

[176] WANDELER, E., THIELE, L., VERHOEF, M., AND LIEVERSE, P. System Architecture Evaluation Using Modular Performance Analysis: A Case Study. *International Journal on Software Tools for Technology Transfer 8*, 6 (2006), 649–667.

[177] WANG, Q., AND SAWHNEY, S. VeCure: A practical security framework to protect the CAN bus of vehicles. In *Internet of Things (IOT), 2014 International Conference on the* (2014), pp. 13–18.

[178] WASICEK, A., DERLER, P., AND LEE, E. A. Aspect-oriented Modeling of Attacks in Automotive Cyber-Physical Systems. In *Proceedings of the 51st Annual Design Automation Conference (DAC)* (USA, 2014), pp. 21:1–21:6.

[179] WILKENS, A. Elektrotaxi EVA für Städte in den Tropen. http://www.heise.de/newsticker/meldung/Elektrotaxi-EVA-fuer-Staedte-in-den-Tropen-2052296.html, 2013. Heise Online.

[180] ZALMAN, R., AND MAYER, A. A Secure but Still Safe and Low Cost Automotive Communication Technique. In *Proceedings of the 51st ACM/EDAC/IEEE Design Automation Conference (DAC)* (USA, 2014), pp. 43:1–43:5.

[181] ZENG, H., DI NATALE, M., GHOSAL, A., AND SANGIOVANNI-VINCENTELLI, A. Schedule Optimization of Time-Triggered Systems Communicating Over the FlexRay Static Segment. *IEEE Transactions on Industrial Informatics 7*, 1 (2011), 1–17.

[182] ZENG, H., GHOSAL, A., AND DI NATALE, M. Timing Analysis and Optimization of FlexRay Dynamic Segment. In *IEEE 10th International Conference on Computer and Information Technology (CIT)* (2010), pp. 1932–1939.

[183] ZENGKUN, F. Electric taxi can go 200km on 15 minute of charging. http://www.straitstimes.com/singapore/electric-taxi-can-go-200km-on-15-minutes-of-charging, 2013. The Straits Times.

[184] ZHU, L., AND TUNG, B. *RFC 4556: Public Key Cryptography for Initial Authentication in Kerberos (PKINIT)*. Request for Comments. IETF, 2006.

[185] ZUBIE INC. Zubie: Get A Connected Car Without Buying A New One. http://zubie.com, 2015. Accessed: 2016-01-19.

List of Tables

List of Figures

Glossary

3DES Triple DES

ABS Anti-lock Braking System

ACL Access Control List

ADAS Advanced Driver Assistance System

AES Advanced Encryption Standard

API Application Programming Interface

ASIL Automotive Safety Integrity Level

AUTOSAR AUTomotive Open System ARchitecture

AVB Audio Video Bridging

BMS Battery Management System

BYOD Bring Your Own Device

CA Certificate Authority

CAN Controller Area Network

CBC Cipher Block Chaining

CFB Cipher Feedback

CIS Central Information Screen

CMAC Cipher-based Message Authentication Code

COTS commercial off-the-shelf

CPU Central Processing Unit

CRC Cyclic Redundancy Check

CREATE Campus for Research Excellence And Technological Enterprise

CRL Certificate Revocation List

CTL Computation Tree Logic

CTMC Continuous-Time Markov Chain

CVSS Common Vulnerability Scoring System

DES Data Encryption Standard

DoS Denial-of-Service

DTMC Discrete Time Markov Chain

ECB Electronic Code Block

ECC Elliptic Curve Cryptography

ECDLP Elliptic Curve Discrete Logarithm Problem

ECU Electronic Control Unit

EDF Earliest Deadline First

ESP Electronic Stability Program

EV Electric Vehicle

FCFS First Come First Serve

FD Flexible Data-Rate

FIBEX Field Bus Exchange Format

FPGA Field Programmable Gate Array

FTDMA Flexible Time Division Multiple Access

FTP File Transfer Protocol

GPS Global Positioning System

GPU Graphics Processing Unit

GUI Graphical User Interface

HD High-Definition

HIL Hardware-in-the-loop

HIS Hersteller Initiative Software

HSM Hardware Security Module

HTTP Hypertext Transfer Protocol

IACS Industrial Automation and Control Systems

IC Instrument Cluster

ID identifier

IDS Intrusion Detection System

IEEE Institute of Electrical and Electronics Engineers

ILP Integer Linear Program

IoT Internet of Things

ISMS Information Security Management System

ISO International Organization for Standardization

IV Initialization Vector

IVNS In-Vehicle Network Simulator

JAR Java Archive

JNI Java Native Interface

JSON JavaScript Object Notation

LASAN Lightweight Authentication for Secure Automotive Networks

Li-Ion Lithium-Ion

LIN Local Interconnect Network

M-MAC Mixed Message Authentication Codes

MAC Message Authentication Code

MAD Median Absolute Deviation

MOST Media Oriented Systems Transport

NFC Near Field Communication

NIST National Institute of Standards and Technology

NIT Network Idle Time

NRF National Research Foundation

OBD On-Board Diagnosis

OCSP Online Certificate Status Protocol

OEM Original Equipment Manufacturer

OPEN One-Pair Ether-Net

OS Operating System

OSI Open Systems Interconnect

OTA Over-The-Air

PDU Protocol Data Unit

PKINIT Public Key Cryptography for Initial Authentication in Kerberos

PUF Physically Unclonable Function

QoS Quality of Service

RAM Random Access Memory

REST Representational State Transfer

RFC Request For Comments

RR Round Robin

RTC Real-Time Calculus

SAAN Security Analysis for Automotive Networks

SeVeCom Secure Vehicle Communication

SHE Secure Hardware Extension

SIL Software-in-the-loop

SMF Shortest Message First

SOA Service Oriented Architecture

SOC state of charge

SOH State of Health

SSL Secure Sockets Layer

TDMA Time Division Multiple Access

TESLA Timed Efficient Stream Loss-Tolerant Authentication

TLS Transport Layer Security

TPM Trusted Platform Module

TSN Time-Sensitive Networking

TUM Technische Universität München

UDP User Datagram Protocol

URL Uniform Resource Locator

USA United States of America

USB Universal Serial Bus

WCRT Worst Case Response Time

XML Extensible Markup Language